D1508175

Raise Your Visibility & Value

Uncover the Lost Art of Connecting on the Job

By Edward Evarts

Published by Motivational Press, Inc.
1777 Aurora Road
Melbourne, Florida, 32935
www.MotivationalPress.com

Manufactured in the United States of America.

ISBN: 978-1-62865-473-8

Contents

PART ONE

FROM NETWORKING AND PERFORMANCE APPRAISALS TO VISIBILITY AND VALUE

PART TWO

RAISE YOUR VISIBILITY

PART THREE
RAISE YOUR VALUE

FREE FOR PURCHASERS OF

RAISE YOUR VISIBILITY & VALUE:

UNCOVER THE LOST ART OF CONNECTING ON THE JOB

Regardless of your age or the tenure of your career, the world of work is changing at an exponential rate. Head-spinning advances in technology, endless bottom-line financial pressures, growing networks of global economies, and changing workplace demographics are significantly impacting your experience in the workplace.

To successfully navigate this changing world of work, business professionals must maximize their visibility within their organization and industry. Hence, insight into activities and behaviors which raise your visibility in your organization and industry becomes a necessity.

This free report, the **Raise Your Visibility Indicator**, simplifies organization and industry visibility by providing you instant insight into areas where visibility comes to life. In addition to gaining insight into areas that currently raise your visibility, you will receive actionable suggestions on how to improve your visibility in areas that warrant your attention.

Congratulations on taking the first step to raise your visibility!

To get your free access, send an email to ed@excellius.com with the tag line "Free Report."

Acknowledgment

"The most important part of your life was the time that you spent with these people.

That's why all of you are here. Nobody does it alone, Jack.

You needed all of them and they needed all of you." [1]

Christian Shepherd to Jack Shepherd,
Lost Television Series, 5/23/2010

Writing a book is a tough journey and not one you can do alone. A sincere thank you to my colleagues who kept me going through their recurring and consistent curiosity on the progress of this book: Karen Burke, Deborah Burkholder, Sarah Mann, and Kathy Maloney, all of whom included, in almost every conversation we had over a five-year period, "How is your book coming along?"

I give a special thank you to Randi Bussin, who suggested and hosted a book editing party at her home, where we were joined by my wonderful colleagues: Suzan Czajkowski, Kathy Evarts, Trisha Griffin-Carty, Kathy Maloney, and Elaine MacLellan.

A very special thank you to my outstanding editor, Sara Murphy, for her dedicated (and very inexpensive) book reading and editing. Sara possesses the skill of providing creative ideas and gentle feedback. I could not have made this journey without her.

And lastly, a special appreciation to my two daughters, Sara and Caroline, and my lovely wife Kathy. They provided me the time and space to get the job done!

Introduction

"The world is changing and changing fast, and frankly, we did not get everything we dreamed of done in the first release," declared Microsoft Vice President Tami Reller, in May 2013, during an unusually frank reflection regarding shortcomings of the recently released Windows 8.[1]

Regardless of your age or the tenure of your career, your organization is changing at an exponential rate. Head-spinning advances in technology, endless bottom-line financial pressures, growing networks of global economies, and changing demographics are significantly impacting your experience in your workplace. Even industry giants like Microsoft have trouble keeping up.

In its never ending effort to stay competitive and solvent, your organization is responding to these technological, financial, global and demographic forces in the following ways:

- **Your organization is treating you like a contractor.** The classic career path is transforming from a linear track, leading from supervisor to vice president, into a series of job assignments – roles that exist within an organization to achieve a defined objective and end once the objective is achieved. You move from role to role and from organization to organization with greater frequency and fluidity than at any previous period in modern management history.

- **Your organization is expecting you to change more frequently.** There was a time when companies were proud of their stability and consistency. Acquisitions were infrequent, co-workers with whom you attended new-hire orientation twenty years earlier were still around to join you for lunch, and a hard day's work provided job security. Today, however, strategies, floor plans, and organization structures are like the secretary in the 1990's sitcom *Murphy Brown* – every day when you come in, a new strategy or floor plan is waiting for you. You and your colleagues are extremely busy and multi-tasking reigns.

- **Your organization needs you to do more with less, and do more, faster.** New technologies are being integrated into your organization to accelerate productivity. Employee turnover is non-stop and when a colleague leaves, her job is frequently not filled and her responsibilities are assigned to others. The pace of change you experience continues to increase as your organization needs to move quickly and nimbly in order to survive. The competitive global marketplace shows little mercy for organizations that are slow to raise the bar for their customers and employees.

- **Your organization is reducing costs by creating virtual work experiences.** The globalization of your organization is creating satellite offices from London to Mumbai. Many of your colleagues work from home as often as they work from the office. Concurrently, your organization is integrating new communication technologies into your workplace to reduce costs and increase efficiencies. Tele-presence meetings and conference calls are negating the necessity to meet in person. The need to be in a virtual relationship is so prolific that a colleague sitting in the cubicle next to you is more likely to send you an email asking if the report you are working on is ready, rather than take a few seconds to walk over and ask you in person. Opportunities for colleagues to interact in person are rapidly diminishing.

- **Your organization is looking for new ways to drive productivity and measure performance.** By all accounts, the classic performance management programs that are prolific in organizations across the globe have failed to deliver on their promise of behavioral change and sustainable results. Rating systems, formats, and categories are so stale that most managers write their appraisals the night before they are due. Many companies like Deloitte, Adobe, and the Gap have significantly modified their performance appraisal processes. What will replace the void that is being created between the urgent need for superior performance and the collapse of performance management systems?

My Beginning

In the winter of 2006, I experienced a change that impacted my career and I, like so many of my colleagues, unexpectedly found myself alone and vulnerable. The change for me came in the form of a new boss, who within minutes of meeting me, looked at me and said, "I don't hear a lot about Ed Evarts in this organization." Until this time, I considered myself a well-performing, highly regarded contributor in my organization. I had received "exceeds expectations" performance appraisals. I was well-known and I thought I had a great reputation. People liked me!

By the spring of 2008, my position was eliminated and my ten-year relationship with my organization came to an end. Buoyed with severance, I took some time to think about my next career move. I was unsure if I wanted to return to a corporate role or make an effort to start a business on my own. I was fortunate to have the benefit of outplacement services, and it was through these services that I was reintroduced to networking.

It had been over ten years since I engaged in any networking activities. Thoughts about how and where to network were unclear. As an employed business professional in a busy, fast-paced organization, I never felt the need or had the time to network. So, like many of my colleagues looking for a job, I began the arduous task of polishing my networking capabilities. I quickly found there was a lot to do.

I attended networking workshops. I sat through networking seminars. I enrolled in networking webinars. I read networking articles and perused networking blogs. I brought my resume up to date, I created cover letters, and I ordered business cards.

I created a LinkedIn profile, a Twitter account, and a Facebook page. To ensure I appeared to be current and active, I updated my LinkedIn profile and I tweeted on a regular basis. I worked to create what networking workshop presenters referred to as my "on-line presence" on Facebook, and strived to maintain my "on-line reputation."

And I practiced, practiced, and practiced. I practiced my thirty-second, one-minute, two-minute and three-minute commercials. I practiced sample interview question responses. I practiced ice breakers designed to jump start a conversation with a person I had just met. Yet, I could not over practice! These same workshop presenters advised participants of the importance of being natural, authentic, and unscripted. Practice... yet be yourself.

INSIGHTS ABOUND

To say I was endlessly networking during the spring and fall of 2008 would be an understatement. The "bottom fell out" of the financial markets in 2008 and by the summer of 2009, a global recession was in full swing. The unemployment rate in the United States increased to 9.5%, with a staggering 14.7 million American workers unemployed.[2]

During the period of my transition, I met individuals actively employed and individuals who found themselves unexpectedly unemployed. Most dramatically, I began to realize a difference between employed business professionals and individuals looking for a job. As I heard more and more stories from my colleagues, I came to the following conclusions regarding their experiences as employed business professionals.

- **You *do not think* about networking while employed.** The idea of connecting with colleagues in your organization or getting to know individuals in your industry is not in your consciousness.

Whether you are dedicated or distracted, your fast-paced, high-stress, multitasking workplace forces the idea of networking into the deep recesses of your brain. Time passes quickly, and by the time a change in your workplace forces you to lift up your head and look around, it is already too late to start networking.

- **If you do think about networking, you spend little time doing so while employed.** Whether it is discomfort, disinterest, or a dearth of time, you are not networking as much as you should be while employed. Imagine not being proficient at something and then starting to work on it when you need it the most. Starting to build your networking skills at the point of a professional change (i.e., reorganization, new boss, and unemployment) is like a golf professional learning to drive a golf ball the day before his debut at the Masters. Any way you slice it, you are already behind before you even begin.

- **You are not skilled at networking.** Whether you are a current or former senior executive, middle manager, or front-line supervisor, your networking skills are lacking. Whether an attorney, sales manager, or human resources business partner, you are unprepared and overwhelmed to network successfully. Whether you consider networking as marketing, self-promotion, or relationship building, you view networking much like getting a root canal – you don't want to do it unless you have to, and it is painful at best.

- **You believe the best way to achieve your professional objective is to network.** Since the recession of 2008, networking has been all the rage. Who could blame underskilled and underprepared individuals, suddenly thrust into a turbulent job market, for rushing into the networking maelstrom? After all, statistics show that 60 – 70% of job opportunities are found through networking.[3] For many individuals, networking not only became a job search activity in addition to posting for open positions and interviewing, but it also became their primary job search activity. How ironic that the predominate strategy for you to achieve your next professional opportunity is an activity at which you are not good at, and on which you spend no time while employed!

- **You mistake good performance with business value.** You have grown up in a culture that measures you from the moment you are born to the moment you retire. The annual performance appraisal process at your organization leads you to believe that being a good performer is enough. Yet, many of you are finding yourself unexpectedly unemployed as business leaders realize that while good performance is acceptable, value creation is better. You continue to overinvest in obtaining an "exceeds expectations" on your annual performance review and underinvest in value creation.

- **To maximize success, you must maximize visibility and value.** The world of work is changing at an exponential rate. These foundational shifts are changing the ways in which you connect with others and achieve your professional goals. If you continue to rely on a deficient definition of networking that does not apply to employed business professionals and if you continue to depend on archaic performance management systems that do not help you create value for your organization, you are missing a more effective and robust strategy with which to achieve your goals.

RAISE YOUR VISIBILITY & VALUE

The conversation I had with my new boss was the first indication which I was, at which time, more alone and vulnerable than I thought. What my new boss was telling me then, which I now understand, is that I was *not visible in my organization*. Sure, I was visible to my colleagues in my department and to my internal clients, but I was not visible beyond that. Compounding my low organizational visibility was that the *value*

I provided to my organization was unknown or worse, non-existent. I was another "heads-down" contributor, focused only on surviving the day and working to ensure I attained an "exceeds expectations" on my next performance appraisal.

You find yourself today just as I found myself then: actively or recently employed, invisible within your organization and industry, and unable to describe the value, if any, you create for your organization.

The goal of this book is to help you, the employed business professional, create individualized strategies to raise your visibility and value in your organization and industry, to move you from being a victim of your organization's environment, and to inspire you to be the catalyst of your own career.

TAKE A MINUTE TO CONSIDER THE FOLLOWING:

- HOW MUCH TIME HAVE YOU SPENT OVER THE LAST THIRTY DAYS RAISING YOUR VISIBILITY WITH YOUR COLLEAGUES AT WORK?

- HOW MUCH TIME HAVE YOU SPENT OVER THE LAST THIRTY DAYS RAISING YOUR VISIBILITY WITH INDIVIDUALS IN YOUR INDUSTRY?

- CAN YOU AND YOUR MANAGER DEFINE HOW VALUE IS MEASURED IN YOUR ORGANIZATION?

- DO YOU KNOW HOW TO DESCRIBE THE VALUE YOU CREATE FOR YOUR ORGANIZATION?

A client of mine, Mike, sums it up beautifully. After a number of years, in a variety of increasingly responsible roles, at one of the largest assisted living providers in North America, Mike was promoted to a senior vice president role. Similar to other organizations across the globe, Mike's company is a fast-paced organization that needs to constantly change and evolve in order to remain cutting-edge and compliant in a highly competitive and regulated industry. As Mike shared with me, "I love my job, my company, and my industry. At the same time, as I reflect back on my career, I can see how easy it is to get caught up in the volume of activity and the pace of change. It is easy to go with the flow and allow your career to unfold naturally, where you are the passenger in a car and your company is the driver. Time passes quickly and at some point, you pick up your head and wonder if you are where you want to be. You realize that you want to take back the 'steering wheel' and take control of your career rather than hope that the next change will benefit you."

Raise Your Visibility & Value changes the way you are viewed in your organization and industry. When you finish reading this book and completing the exercises found at the end of certain chapters, you will:

- Realize that networking as you define it today is no longer enough for you to achieve your professional objectives.

- Understand that performance management systems hinder your career growth and your ability to differentiate yourself within your organization.

- Create activities that will help you move beyond networking and raise your visibility in your organization and industry.

- Create activities that will help you avoid the limitations of performance appraisals and raise your value in your organization.

- Increase your satisfaction in the work that you do and your engagement in your organization's goals and mission.

Let's begin the journey.

PART ONE

From Networking and Performance Appraisals to Visibility and Value

CHAPTER ONE

Why Networking and Performance Appraisals Are Not Enough

SUSAN'S STORY

Each morning, Susan, a former call center manager, rises to face a new day of job search activities. Unexpectedly unemployed, Susan needs to find a job for reasons that would not surprise anyone – money, benefits, and a feeling of contribution.

Like so many others who are between jobs, Susan is doing the following activities to find her next opportunity:

- Posting for jobs online
- Chasing down recruiters
- Leaving messages with hiring managers
- Networking

Occasionally, she connects with a recruiter, participates in a phone screen, or sits face-to-face with a hiring manager.

As time passes, these activities begin to feel increasingly repetitive and Susan's energy level begins to drop. Searching for a job is hard! Where should Susan focus her energy in order to benefit from the largest return on her investment? All of her colleagues who are unemployed talk endlessly about networking, so there must be something to it. Thus, Susan attends networking events and mingles with other business professionals. She contacts former co-workers to seek their assistance. Susan follows up with individuals she has met while networking to see how she and this individual can help each other. Susan focuses all of her efforts networking, as she has heard that most of her unemployed colleagues found their current jobs through someone they knew. Susan is optimistic that her next opportunity is right around the corner.

CARL'S STORY

Carl is one of several in-house attorneys for a software development company that has exploded over the past few years, and has a busy day ahead of him. He has several meetings to attend, a handful of conference calls to join, critical work to complete, and one or two personal errands to run. By the time Carl arrives at his office and puts artificial sweetener and lactose-free soy milk in his coffee, he is already behind schedule.

As Carl's workday ends, he takes a moment to reflect on his day. He moved so quickly between meetings, he barely had time to greet colleagues he passed in the hall. Carl rode the elevator with the new Vice President of Sales. "Hi, Kevin," she said as Carl entered the elevator. "Hi, Mandy," Carl replied. (Her name is Mary.) Carl made progress on work he needed to complete, yet his progress came with a cost – other than the meetings and conference calls he attended and a few moments to grab lunch at the local deli, he never left his desk. Carl realizes if there were a calendar for workers who represent a "heads-down" mentality, he would be Mr. November. The day feels like so many others.

Time passes and one day Carl's boss calls him into the office to introduce him to three new attorneys who are joining the organization due to a recent acquisition. Carl's boss is brimming with excitement, anticipating the fresh perspectives and untapped value his newest team members will bring.

At home that evening, once the news has sunk in, Carl begins to wonder if he is viewed as a contributor who provides fresh perspectives and organizational value. Carl struggles to articulate the value he provides and realizes that if he can't, his boss probably can't. As a contributor with a history of "exceeds expectations" performance reviews, Carl wonders if his inability to articulate his value matters anyway. As he continues to think about himself in the organization, he realizes that the colleagues he passes in the hall, the co-workers with whom he attends meetings, and the executives with whom he occasionally rides the elevator *see* him, but don't *know* him. As his newly acquired colleagues begin to entrench themselves in the organization, Carl realizes that he should have thought about his visibility and value a lot earlier.

ELAINE'S STORY

Elaine loves being a self-employed website designer and content manager. She gets to do the work she enjoys, which illustrates her natural graphic and design talents. She is able to set her own hours and work with a variety of interesting clients and challenging projects. If she could, Elaine would design websites all day. Elaine recognizes that when it comes to generating revenue, every day is a new beginning. In order to sustain her business month over month and year over year, she must have multiple prospects waiting in the wings.

Being self-employed requires a tremendous amount of time and energy. Not only does Elaine do all of the design work, she has to track her expenses, pay her bills, shop for office supplies, solve computer problems, speak with clients, and prospect for new business. Like so many of her colleagues, Elaine is technically efficient in her field, yet less efficient prospecting for new opportunities and marketing the value she provides her customers. Marketing, prospecting, and selling feel like a full-time job.

Fortunately for Elaine, most of her business comes through referrals. Elaine tries to focus as much as she can on networking as she knows that people need to know her in order to refer her. Elaine is optimistic that her networking efforts will pay off.

THEIR STORY

One day while enjoying a dinner at their favorite restaurant, Susan, her husband Carl, and her sister, Elaine, share highlights from their respective days. While their days are wildly different, as their discussion unfolds, it becomes increasingly apparent that a set of activities are common between Susan and Elaine. To achieve their professional goals, each of them spends a lot of time networking.

For Susan, her goal is to land a job; for Elaine, to obtain revenue. Susan is looking to make new connections and to secure references. Elaine is looking to make new connections and obtain referrals.

Yet, where is Carl in this discussion? Is he so mesmerized by his delicious veal parmigiana dinner that his attention is focused elsewhere? Perhaps Carl is keeping a low profile during this discussion because, like so many employed business professionals, he does not think networking applies to him. "I'm employed! Who needs networking?" Carl is so busy navigating his way through a daily barrage of emails, meetings, and deadlines, whether he is in his office, or elsewhere, he barely has time to think. And the last thing he is going to think about is his annual performance assessment.

THE ORIGINS OF NETWORKING

There is little doubt that human beings have a need for social interaction. In his landmark paper *A Theory of Human Motivation* (1943), Abraham Maslow concluded that, after fulfilling our psychological and safety needs, we must fulfill our interpersonal and "belongingness" needs. To paraphrase Maslow, individuals hunger for affectionate relationships with people and they will strive with great intensity to achieve this goal.[1]

I could attempt to impress you with my sophisticated research skills about human motivation and needs, but all you have to do is take a look in a mirror and you are very likely to see someone who longs to be needed and connected to others.

One popular activity to satisfy our hunger, find our place in a group, and connect with others is networking. Networking is not a recent phenomenon. I am confident that ancient Romans found time to gather in a public place, share a goblet of wine, and talk about the important topics of the day. From my research, it appears that most networking in ancient Rome took place outdoors. This all changed, of course, with the advent of the hotel. Once the Courtyard by Marriott was invented, networkers finally found a place to gather, unencumbered by obstacles like unexpected thunderstorms and packs of wild animals. Gathered close together in the Presidential Ballroom, networkers now enjoy cash bars, restroom sinks that allow you to wash your hands without touching anything, and name badges.

Today, networking is omnipresent. In an effort to connect with others, your colleagues will:

- Attend teleclasses and webinars hosted by nationally known networking experts.
- Participate in workshops focused on methods to network.
- Read books on networking.
- Devour articles written by world-class networkers.
- View blogs by the same world-class networkers, who have re-purposed the aforementioned articles (re-purposing is like re-gifting, without the scotch tape).
- Talk about how they *should be* networking, yet never do any actual networking.
- Attend networking events,
- ... and more networking events,
- ... and even more networking events.

You frequently hear that networking is a critical activity for your professional success. I know I did when I attended the dozens of workshops, webinars, teleclasses, and networking events during my transition from my last employer. If you are an individual in transition like Susan, or a self-employed business professional like Elaine, you need to focus a significant portion of your time and energy networking. Nothing will get an individual in transition or working to develop business in front of a decision maker faster than a network introduction.

WHAT ARE THE BENEFITS OF NETWORKING?

Networking is and will continue to be an important professional activity for business professionals. I previously stated that 60 - 70% of employed individuals located their most recent job opportunity through networking. In a poll I conducted on LinkedIn, these numbers were corroborated when 59% of 1,339 respondents chose the category "by networking with friends and colleagues" as the strategy that led them to their most recent job.[2] Therefore, networking seems to be three times more effective than using an on-line job board and almost three times more effective than using a recruiter.

Similarly, self-employed business owners*, like Elaine, state that 95% of their business opportunities come from networking.[3] Whether you are seeking a web designer, an accountant or a mechanic, you will almost always pick up the phone or email a friend or colleague and ask for a referral.

For business professionals looking for their next job or self-employed business owners seeking revenue, networking has many benefits. When networking, these individuals can:

- Practice how they verbally and visually present themselves to others.
- Polish how they describe their goals, needs, and capabilities.

---

*Note: when I mention "self-employed business owners," I am generally describing privately owned, one-to-two person businesses which are primarily selling a service. I am not referring to businesses selling one or more products or larger service providers who possess other methods to market their services (i.e., social media, newspaper/magazine ads, and cars and trucks personalized with their logo).

- Meet colleagues who can introduce them to others who can help them.

- Connect with colleagues whose work complements their own, creating new synergies and opportunities.

- Hear what others are doing which may generate new ideas for them.

- Try out new looks in their wardrobe, ensuring it is polished, up-to-date, and ready for interviews and meetings.

- Create opportunities for others to give them feedback on what they are doing that works and what they are doing that could improve.

- Catch up with old friends and be reminded that they are not alone.

By and far, networking is the most effective strategy for business professionals to land a job and self-employed business owners to generate revenue.

WHY IS NETWORKING BECOMING INCREASINGLY INEFFECTIVE FOR EMPLOYED BUSINESS PROFESSIONALS?

While networking is the most effective strategy for individuals looking to land a new job and for self-employed business owners to generate revenue, networking is significantly less effective for employed business professionals who are seeking ways to grow within their current organization, as illustrated in Figure 1.1.

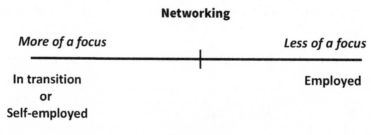

Figure 1.1

Carl is not networking within his organization, nor does he intend to. Although he needs to do something in order to raise his visibility and value, he, as an employed business professional, does not need to resort to networking activities that work so well for his colleagues who are looking for a job or working to generate revenue. If you think networking is the best way to get promoted, expand your influence, and become more valuable to your organization, you will be very disappointed.

For individuals like Carl, the real perpetrator that is stifling value creation in your organization is not your job description – it is the performance appraisal.

WHY IS THE PERFORMANCE APPRAISAL BECOMING INCREASINGLY INEFFECTIVE FOR EMPLOYED BUSINESS PROFESSIONALS?

History will not be kind to the performance appraisal. After decades of lackluster experiences, stale formats, and non-existent correlations between assessment and achievement, most savvy business leaders and modern management experts would tell you that the performance appraisal is a well-intended yet failed exercise in behavior modification. In a 2014 survey of 1,480 business professionals, an astounding 76% of participants gave their organizations a "C" or worse on the way it conducts its performance appraisal process; 25% gave their organization a "D" or worse.[4] Like the abacus, typewriter, and that sound you heard when you connected to a modem, the performance appraisal should be immediately shipped to the Museum of Outdated Business Artifacts.

The most egregious component of the performance appraisal experience is the bell curve. In organizations primarily focused on managing their budgets or obsessed with structure and process, a bell curve is a convenient tool used to dictate the percentage of employees who have to fall into a particular rating category, as illustrated in Figure 1.2. No tool could be more "anti-value" than the bell curve. Why? Since the performance bell curve predetermines how many employees must fall into each category, your organization's culture is encouraging you to spend all of your time (one of the assets needed to create value) avoiding the dreaded "below" and "does not meet" performance appraisal ratings rather than focusing on how to create value in your organization.

THE ANTI-VALUE BELL CURVE

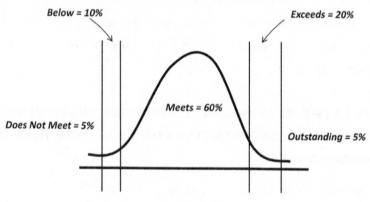

Figure 1.2

While we love positive feedback, we don't love being assessed. There is something palpably uncomfortable about sitting in an office, hearing a recap of your exhaustive and tiring efforts over the prior year distilled down into a rating of 1 to 5. Despite the fact that 99.9% of the world's population would do anything other than participate in the performance appraisal process, the performance appraisal continues to survive.[5] Clever advocates have tried to deflect the criticism of performance appraisals by giving them new names like the performance assessment or performance calibration. Creative technologists have built snazzy online platforms that self-generate standardized comments and allow multiple raters to provide input. Capable Human Resource leaders have broadened the role of the performance appraisal by integrating it into a larger "performance management system." However, as the old saying goes, you can put lipstick on a pig but it is still a pig. Not that I am associating pigs with performance appraisals – surveys have proven that people like pigs more.[6]

How do you know if your organization has a performance management system? I think you know, as your body is already starting to shudder. Once a year, your boss is thrust into the dreaded "performance management cycle" and required to complete numerous performance appraisals. As he rushes to complete his appraisals en masse the Sunday night before the appraisals are due, his ratings are influenced by the rankings and bell-curve pre-established by your organization. Upon the completion of an exhausting approval process, he finally schedules a meeting with you. Following the meeting, you rush back to your cubicle, call your significant other and exclaim, "I got a 3.5 on collaboration!"

Your reaction is not your fault. You have grown up in a culture built around performance management, rating categories, and numerical rankings. If you took a moment to reflect on your life, you would recall statements similar to the following:

- **Your wonder-filled days as an infant.** "Your daughter is in the 98th percentile for height and the 95th percentile for weight."

- **Your wistful days as a teenager.** "Your daughter has received an A in History, a B+ in Social Sciences, and an A- in Biology."

- **Your wild days as a collegiate.** "Please notify your parents that your cumulative grade point average at the completion of your sophomore year is 3.25."

It is no wonder that, by the time you enter the workplace, you are fully expecting the apex of your career to be best described as "4.2."

The times, however, are changing. Employers from across the globe are tiring of this aging method for measuring and communicating performance. If performance management systems were a currency in today's financial markets, they would be downgraded to a point of worthlessness. The words are archaic, the numbers are impersonal, and the performance appraisal's ability to positively modify behavior is underwhelming.

Networking while employed and your dependency on performance appraisals are becoming increasingly ineffective because of the following growing areas of interest:

- The frequency of change in your organization
- The pace of change in your organization
- The increase of professional transparency in your organization
- The reduction of energy

What is Meant by the Frequency of Change in Your Organization?

Frequency refers to *how often* change occurs. There was a time when organizations were proud of their stability and consistency. Acquisitions were infrequent, and words like "right-sizing" and "down-sizing" were not in the dictionary. Your job description had not changed for years.

Today, mergers and acquisitions are a daily event. Yesterday's technology upgrades quickly become obsolete. Roles, responsibilities, and relationships change faster than a name plate on a cubicle. If you are like so many others in your organization, you have had three to five bosses in the past five years. Kevin, a client, shared with me that the boss with whom he wrote his annual goals was not, for three years running, the same boss who reviewed his achievement to his goals at the end of the year. A new year, a new boss; a new boss, a new set of expectations.

In a March 2014 poll conducted by *Inc.* magazine, 28% of the respondents' business models changed in the last five years; 36% of the respondents' mix of products and services changed; and 47% of the respondents' financial structure changed.[7] I frequently speak with clients who have received emails that a workgroup – for example, Account Management – has reorganized its staff and function, effective immediately. These same clients attest that it feels like the same workgroup just reorganized six months earlier! I worked with a client company whose leadership and organizational structure was relatively the same for almost *forty years*. This same organization has changed its leadership and "go-to-market" structure three times in the last *six years*.

Take a moment to think about the answer to the following question.

IN THE PAST FIVE YEARS, HOW FREQUENTLY HAS MY ORGANIZATION CHANGED SOMETHING THAT SIGNIFICANTLY IMPACTS ITS EMPLOYEES OR ITS CUSTOMERS?

WHAT IS MEANT BY THE PACE OF CHANGE IN YOUR ORGANIZATION?

The second reason networking and performance appraisals are becoming increasingly ineffective for employed business professionals is **pace** or *how quickly* you are expected to change. You are being asked to do more with less, and do more, faster. Listen to Virginia Rometty, the Chief Executive Officer for IBM. The headline of a *Wall Street Journal* article published in April 2013 boldly declares "IBM's Chief to Employees: Think Fast, Move Faster."[8] With so many changes occurring within your industry and markets, your organization needs you to change faster. Reporting structures announced today are effective *next Monday*. The enterprise-wide telecom platform upgrade announced last Tuesday feels as though it is going live tomorrow. A high-tech company that began operations two years ago suddenly has a multi-million or billion dollar valuation. The social media darling Instagram was launched in October 2010 and sold in April 2012 to Facebook for one *billion* dollars. It took forty-two years for television to have 50 million users. The iPod? *Just three years.*[9]

Take a moment to think about the answers to the following questions as they relate to changes at your organization.

> WHAT ARE SOME CHANGES THAT HAVE BEEN ANNOUNCED
> RECENTLY AT YOUR ORGANIZATION?
>
> WHAT IS THE TIME FRAME BETWEEN WHEN THE CHANGES WERE
> ANNOUNCED AND THE DATE THE CHANGES WERE SCHEDULED TO
> TAKE EFFECT?

WHAT IS MEANT BY PROFESSIONAL TRANSPARENCY IN YOUR ORGANIZATION?

The third reason networking while employed and performance appraisals are becoming increasingly ineffective is the explosive growth in **professional transparency**. As recently as seven years ago, unless the subject of your search was your favorite movie star, rock star, or politician, your ability to find details about another individual was challenging. This was not due to your faulty research skills - information about an average individual simply did not exist publicly. In fact, information about others was so absent in the not-too-distant past, the thought of seeking out personal or professional details regarding another person would not have even occurred to you.

Today, individuals you have never met, from anywhere on the globe, are instantly finding out more about you than any other time in human history. Whether individuals are at their desk in a towering glass office building, sequestered in their basement at their suburban home, or lounging at their favorite cappuccino bar, individuals can instantly access volumes of information about you with only a few keystrokes. Fortunately, some of this information is beneficial to your profile; unfortunately, some of this is decidedly not.

Recently, I attended a social media presentation that was hosted by the president of a regional marketing organization. To show the power of Google, one of his colleagues googled the president's name as the president was speaking, and a lot of information appeared behind him on a screen. Unfortunately, one of the items on the screen was a link to a court document detailing his recent divorce. Although it was in clear view to the audience, this leader never turned around to see the link and his colleague never said a word. I doubt that this is information he would have chosen as a backdrop during his presentation!

At the same time, you are able to tell people about yourself with greater ease than ever before. If you go back a few short years, before Facebook and Google, the ways to share information about your accomplishments and background were limited to a resume. Your primary strategy was face-to-face, one-by-one conversations with others. Transparency was low. With technology like Facebook, Google, LinkedIn, and YouTube, you have the ability to increase your personal and professional transparency and instantly share information about yourself with millions of people – all with just a few clicks on a keyboard.

At the same time, organizations across the globe are seeking ways to increase employee transparency. Technology is providing organizations the ability to build internal platforms (à la Facebook and LinkedIn) that allow their employees to build a profile and share information about themselves that are critical to the business. Employees can post a picture, and list their competencies, certifications, degrees, sample projects, work history, and interests. Internal decision makers, hiring managers, and colleagues can subsequently mine for talent internally before looking externally.

As a busy business professional, Carl takes little time to connect with others and his employer is not waiting for him to find the time to do so. His employer is already taking steps to increase Carl's professional transparency, whether Carl likes it or not.

WHERE DOES YOUR ENERGY GO?

The last reason networking while employed and performance appraisals are both becoming increasingly ineffective is that your work environment is busy, frenzied, and overwhelming. In today's fast-paced and fast-changing organizations, where you are being asked to do more with less, and do more, faster, who has time to network? Who has the time to proactively work on their performance assessment categories? You are more focused on keeping up with the changes at your organization than you are on your career. You are doing the job of two people and you end your day with more things to do than when you started your day. Your Outlook calendar is double and triple booked. Your workday flies by faster than a jet soaring across the sky at the speed of sound. Some days it feels as though you are both sacrificing your career on your organization's altar of activity.

A day rarely goes by without a co-worker saying:

- "Is it 5:00 already?"
- "Can you imagine it is (insert month) already?"
- "Is the year really almost over?"
- "Where does the time go?"

If your workday is so busy, what about after work or on the weekend? It is safe to say that due to personal commitments or pure exhaustion, the last thing you want to do is hang around the lobby of a Courtyard by Marriott, wearing a stick-on nametag that never seems to stay stuck, and exchange business cards with a bunch of strangers.

What Professional Risks Do Change and Transparency Create For You?

The frequency and pace of change in your organization, the exponential growth of your professional transparency, your lack of energy to connect with others while employed (visibility), and your lack of energy regarding your performance assessment (value), all create professional risks for you. With increased turbulence in your organization resulting in roles, responsibilities, and relationships changing with great frequency, your ability to benefit from the development of organic relationships (ones that grow naturally over time) or purposeful relationships (ones that you proactively create with a goal in mind) is being seriously eroded. Suddenly, you are at risk of:

- Missing an opportunity to be promoted.
- Being overlooked for increased responsibilities in your current role.
- Being overlooked as a candidate for a visible short-term assignment.
- Missing professional opportunities for reassignment to a new role during an organizational restructuring.
- Being adversely impacted by a layoff.
- Losing control of your reputation.

Allyn Gardner, a coach at Harvard Business School's career program for MBA students and President of Brookside Consulting Partners, has worked with hundreds of business professionals. "Business professionals are so focused on the day-to-day of the business that they rarely take into account what is coming around the corner for their careers," says Allyn. "Many business professionals, even those in their thirties and forties, are reacting rather than planning ahead. They respond to whatever trigger someone else pulls, whether it is an acquisition of the business, a change in the business model, or a corporate restructuring."

Like a picturesque coast line slowly eroding, time passes so quickly at your organization that you don't realize how much ground you have lost until it is too late.

IS IT TOO LATE FOR CARL?

The good news is that it is not too late for Carl... or you. You can use your recognition of the frequency and pace of change at your organization, your knowledge of the exponential increase of your professional transparency, and higher energy regarding raising your visibility and value in new ways to help your career grow and prosper.

In the following chapters, you will be introduced to a strategy that will raise your visibility and value in your organization and industry. By raising your visibility and value, you will:

- Increase your likelihood for promotion, new responsibilities, and career growth.

- Navigate your organization more effectively, increasing your relevance, influence, and impact.

- Build relationships that matter by collaborating with colleagues to solve problems and manage change.

- Facilitate progress more easily by helping your organization achieve its mission, goals, and strategies.

- Experience greater job satisfaction.

Chapter One Recap

- Networking is a very effective activity for you if you are looking for a job or if you are a self-employed business owner looking for revenue.

- When networking, you can:

  - Practice how you verbally and visually present yourself to others.

  - Polish how you describe your goals, needs, and capabilities.

  - Meet colleagues who can introduce you to others who can help you.

  - Connect with colleagues whose work complements your own, which will create new synergies and opportunities.

  - Hear what others are doing which may generate new ideas for you.

  - Try out new looks in your wardrobe, ensuring it is polished, up-to-date, and ready for interviews and meetings.

  - Create opportunities for others to give you feedback on what you are doing that works and what you are doing that could improve.

  - Catch up with old friends.

  - Be reminded that you are not alone.

- Performance appraisals are a poor tool for identifying value and valuable employees within an organization.

- Networking and performance appraisals are becoming increasingly ineffective due to:

  - The frequency of change and how often change occurs.

  - The pace of change and how quickly you are expected to change.

- The increase of professional transparency in your organization.

- The absence of time to network.

- These unaddressed changes in your organization are creating professional risks for you in a variety of ways, including:

  - Missing an opportunity to be promoted.

  - Being overlooked for increased responsibilities in your current role.

  - Being overlooked as a candidate for a visible short-term assignment.

  - Missing professional opportunities for reassignment to a new role during an organizational restructuring.

  - Being adversely impacted by a layoff.

  - Losing control of your reputation.

- It is not too late for you! You can make great progress in your career by focusing more of your time and effort on raising your visibility and value.

CHAPTER TWO

Raise Your Visibility & Value

As Susan and Elaine grab their business cards and head out to their next networking event, Carl begins to realize he needs to kick things into high gear, yet in a different way. As an employed business professional, in order to make progress in your career in today's fast-paced and competitive business environments, Carl and you need new activities and strategies. Continuing to invest in activities that fit another era is not an effective use of your time. Albert Einstein is credited with saying, "If you want different results, do not do the same things." With all due respect to Albert, it does not take a genius to know that your fast-paced and fast-changing organization demands that you do things differently in order to obtain different results. In particular, you both need to reject the classic definition of networking (which we will explore shortly), and invest in activities that are different from what your colleagues in transition and building a business are doing to succeed.

Before getting into the nuts and bolts of the *Raise Your Visibility & Value* model, Carl and you first need to change how you think about connecting with others.

WHAT IS RAISE YOUR VISIBILITY & VALUE ALL ABOUT?

Research tells us that how we define something dictates the activities we subscribe to it. There is a famous example from the turn of the 19th century that illustrates this point. In an effort to change how the public perceived his company, the president of a railroad company declared,

"We are not a train company - we are a transportation company!" Suddenly, by viewing his organization as a provider of transportation and not just an owner of trains, he created new customer perspectives and business opportunities.

If the way we define something dictates the activities that we attach to it, we are at risk of using a definition that limits us. In my workshops, I use the following exercise to help participants understand how their definition of something limits their point of view.

Take a moment to think about and jot down your definition of networking.

NETWORKING IS_____

In my workshops, the vast majority of participants define networking in the following way. See how your response compares.

"TWO INDIVIDUALS MEETING TO SHARE INFORMATION THAT WILL HELP THE OTHER PERSON, EITHER NOW OR IN THE FUTURE."

Was your response similar? If the words are different, is your definition comparable in theme? Do you share some of the key words like "individuals," "information," and "help"?

Set your definition of networking aside for a few moments – we will come back to it later.

Next, take a moment to look at the following picture. Most of you will recognize it as a picture of George Washington.

Take just a few seconds to complete the following statement with the first thought that pops into your head.

MOST PEOPLE WOULD THINK OF GEORGE WASHINGTON AS

_____

When I ask for the phrases that participants identified, they usually include:

- Father of our country
- First president of the United States
- Commander-in-chief
- The guy on the one dollar bill
- The guy who cut down the cherry tree (yes, every workshop has a comedian)

What was your response? If you are like 90% of the participants in my workshops, you thought of one of the first three phrases, and very likely one of the first two.

Next, take a moment to answer the following question. "When you think of George Washington as the father of our country or the first president of the United States, what are some tangible activities in which George would engage when performing these roles?" Tangible activities may include activities such as "make a speech," or "sign a bill." They do not include activities such as "inspire" or "lead," which are intangible. Write in some of your thoughts below.

Common responses among workshop participants include:

- Sign bills into law
- Lead the army
- Meet foreign dignitaries
- Speak to constituents
- Preside over Congress
- Host dinners
- Make speeches

Set your list of George Washington activities aside for a moment and answer the following question (this one is a little tricky). "What is the *broadest definition* you can think of to describe George Washington?"

GEORGE WASHINGTON IS _____

After a few shout-outs by some brave souls willing to get early answers wrong, someone in the audience eventually says "a man" (which is a broader definition than Father of our Country). This response eventually leads to "a human being," which is arguably the broadest way to think about George without getting too existential. What was your response to this question? Were you broad enough in your view of George?

Now, let's think of George Washington as a human being. What are some tangible activities in which George would participate as a human being? Think of your responses in contrast to your earlier thoughts when we were thinking of George as the first President of the United States, and write them below.

If you are like the majority of individuals who have completed this exercise concerning George Washington as a human being, you thought of activities similar to the following:

- Farm his land
- Have dinner with Martha
- Ride his horse
- Sleep
- Eat
- Drink
- Sign bills into law

- Travel with friends
- Do chores around the house
- Buy land
- Smoke a pipe
- Make speeches
- Spend time with his children

Defining George as a human being will generate an endless list of activities. To illustrate the hypothesis that how we define something dictates the activities we subscribe to it, this exercise consistently demonstrates the following:

- The activities that individuals assign to a person, place or thing are limited by the way the person, place, or thing is defined.
- When we define a person, place, or thing in the broadest way, a more extensive list of activities will be generated.

It is interesting to point out that in the dozens of times I have overseen this exercise, no one has ever yelled out "man" or "human being" upon first seeing the picture of George.

What does this exercise tell us? Recall the definition of networking to which the vast majority of participants in my workshops subscribe and to which you may also subscribe.

> "TWO INDIVIDUALS MEETING TO SHARE INFORMATION THAT WILL HELP THE OTHER PERSON, EITHER NOW OR IN THE FUTURE."

When you take a few moments to assign activities to this definition of networking, your list may look similar to the following:

- Meet another individual.
- Meet in person (i.e., at a coffee shop), by phone, or via Skype.
- Share information.
- Share leads.
- Provide information and leads that help the other person.

That's it! This common definition of networking and the limited number of activities which can be assigned to the definition is the core challenge for busy business professionals working to survive in fast-paced and fast-changing organizations. This definition does not reflect the environment in which you work, and it is too limiting in the activities it creates.

In order to maximize the activities in which you can participate as you work to increase your impact at work, a new definition for networking is needed. Consider putting your old definition of networking aside and apply the following new definition.

> **NETWORKING** IS ANY ACTIVITY THAT RAISES MY VISIBILITY AND VALUE IN MY ORGANIZATION AND INDUSTRY.

By using this definition, your mindset changes and your focus shifts to a broader set of activities that raise your visibility and value in your organization and industry. With this definition, you infuse activities into your current workday that raise your visibility among decision makers, without adding more activities into your already busy day. With this definition, you ensure that the work that you do adds value to what is important to your organization. You will not be doing busy work that leaves you physically and mentally drained and feeling undervalued. With this definition, you increase your success at work.

How Do Visibility and Value Relate to Each Other?

It is important to recognize that visibility and value are deeply embedded in your organization and industry. You already know that professional risks exist for busy business professionals who are invisible or undervalued in their organization. You do not want to be visible without providing value, and it is hard to demonstrate the value that you provide if you are invisible.

To better understand how visibility, value, and risk intersect in the workplace, consider the information illustrated in Figure 2.1.

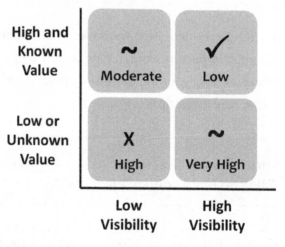

Figure 2.1

- **Low or Unknown Value + Low Visibility.** You are at a **high risk level** when a headcount reduction or departmental realignment occurs. The only reason you might survive is that no one knows what you do or where to find you!

- **Low or Unknown Value + High Visibility.** You are at a **very high risk level,** as you are providing little value and everyone knows it. How have you survived this far?

- **High and Known Value + Low Visibility.** You are at a **moderate risk level,** as the value you are providing exists – decision makers just don't know who you are.

- **High and Known Value + High Visibility.** You are at a **low risk level,** as you are providing value to, and are visible in your organization and industry. While no one can guarantee you employment or a promotion, you are reducing the likelihood of unexpectedly losing your job or missing a promotion.

Your journey to *Raise Your Visibility & Value* will differ from your colleagues. You may feel that you are very visible in your organization, yet your value is unclear. Or, you and your organization may know the value that you provide the organization, yet not a lot of decision makers know who you are.

Take a moment, using Figure 2.2, to complete the following steps:

1. Draw a dot (●) at the place that you feel best represents your *current level* of visibility and value in your **organization**.

2. Draw a star (★) at the place that you feel best represents your *current level* of visibility and value in your **industry.**

3. Draw a dot (●) at the place where you want your level of visibility and value in your **organization** to be.

4. Draw a star (★) at the place where you want your level of visibility and value in your **industry** to be.

5. Draw a line connecting the two dots and draw a second line connecting the two stars.

YOUR ORGANIZATION AND INDUSTRY VISIBILITY AND VALUE

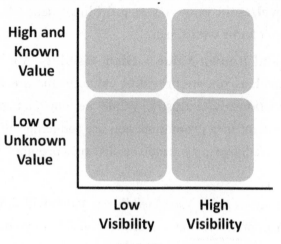

Figure 2.2

These two lines represent your personal journey raising your visibility and value. As you continue reading *Raise Your Visibility & Value,* consider where you need to focus the majority of your energy in order to create strategies that will impact your career most effectively. Perhaps you need to focus on visibility. Perhaps you need to focus on value. If you are like the majority of employed business professionals who are striving to survive their fast-paced and fast-changing organizations, you will need to focus on raising your visibility *and* your value.

Chapter Two Recap

- To make progress in your career in today's competitive organizations, new activities and strategies are needed for employed business professionals.
- Continuing to invest in activities that fit another era or are not proving to be productive is not an effective use of your time.
- High and known value and low visibility means folks don't know who you are.
- The way individuals looking for a job and self-employed business owners define networking – "Two individuals meeting to share information that will help the other person, either now or in the future" – is becoming increasingly ineffective for employed business professionals.
- How you define something dictates the activities that you assign to it. If your definition is limited (i.e., George Washington as the "father of our country" versus a "human being"), you will think of fewer activities.
- Redefine networking as "any activity that raises my visibility *and* value in my organization and industry."
- Visibility, value, and risk are intertwined in your organization and industry.
    - Low or unknown value and low visibility create high professional risk.
    - Low or unknown value and high visibility create very high professional risk.
    - High and known value and low visibility means folks don't know who you are.
    - High and known value and high visibility means you are providing value to, and are visible in, your organization and industry.

PART TWO

Raise Your Visibility

CHAPTER THREE

Raise Your Visibility

You have read a lot so far about your changing organization and the new way to look at creating a successful career for yourself that is more productive and effective – *Raise Your Visibility & Value*. Now it is time to delve deeper into the first part of the formula – **visibility.**

When I think about the growing importance of visibility in the workplace, I think about a client of mine, Eric, who at the time of our conversation was the Vice President of Operations for a global business-to-business services company. During our first session, Eric sounded pretty depressed as he shared with me his need to raise his visibility in his organization. Eric had been at his organization for over twenty years, which represented most of his professional career.

A month or so earlier, a colleague of Eric's, with whom he had been working to improve operational efficiencies associated with a specific client interface, had an opportunity to meet with the president of their division to provide her with an update on the project. "When my colleague called me to update me on the meeting," Eric confided, "he not only shared that the president was pleased with our progress, but when my colleague mentioned my name, the president asked, 'Who's Eric?'" Eric sighed on the phone. "I mistakenly equated tenure and title with visibility. I was wrong."

Eric is not alone. I have talked with many business professionals for whom their degree of visibility in their organization is either unknown or not what they think it is.

WHAT IS VISIBILITY?

You live and work in an increasingly transparent world, yet you find yourself less visible within your organization. You live and work in a time where the ways you can connect with one another are endless, yet you feel less connected with your colleagues. It seems counterintuitive, doesn't it?

When you think about it, this experience should not be too surprising. You can connect with colleagues in so many ways that do not require your physical presence; connecting by actually being physically present seems so "yesterday." Emails, texts, tweets, updates, voice messages, and statuses seem like the preferred way to connect in fast-paced and frenetic work environments. Who has time to leave their office? Why go to the office when you can accomplish so much from your car? Why get in your car if you have the ability to work from your home? What's next? - Avatars that represent you on video calls while you catch a few extra minutes of sleep? You can just feel your visibility being slowly sucked away by a virtual vacuum.

In the *Raise Your Visibility & Value* model:

> **VISIBLE** IS BEING SEEN AND KNOWN WITHIN YOUR ORGANIZATION AND INDUSTRY IN WAYS THAT ADVANCE YOUR CAREER.

You do not realize it as it is happening **and** you spend little time working to raise your visibility at your workplace. When I ask colleagues, clients, and workshop participants to think about why so little time is spent raising their visibility, I commonly hear one of the following responses:

- "I do not have the time."
- "I do not need to."
- "It is too hard."

I am reminded of an anecdote shared with me by Sarah, a colleague at a global business-to-business services organization that I mentioned earlier. Her company has been around for more than fifty years, yet historically, they have not experienced a lot of change. Over the past six years, however, they have navigated through three significant reorganizations in response to economic and market pressures. In the midst of these many changes, Sarah found herself surprised by the number of employees who indicated that during these times of transition they were keeping their heads down. "People seemed to think that 'flying under the radar' was somehow going to ensure, or at least increase, the likelihood of job security."

This heads-down mentality is prevalent in organizations across the globe. Busy business professionals rationalize, even during times of great upheaval and change, that they don't have the time or don't need to raise their visibility. They believe that keeping a low profile equates to high stability.

Conversely, now, more than ever, being visible is critical to your long-term success in your fast-moving, ever-changing organization.

When you think about being visible, consider that there are three levels of visibility: low, medium, and high, as illustrated in Figure 3.1. The two levels that typically impact your visibility are your *personal visibility* and the *visibility of the work that you do.*

Low Visibility

- You are **unseen,** and the work that you do is **unknown** to colleagues outside of your functional area and organizational leaders who can positively influence your career.

Medium Visibility

- You are **seen,** and the work that you do is **known** to your boss, colleagues in your functional area, and some colleagues outside of your functional area.

LEVELS OF VISIBILITY

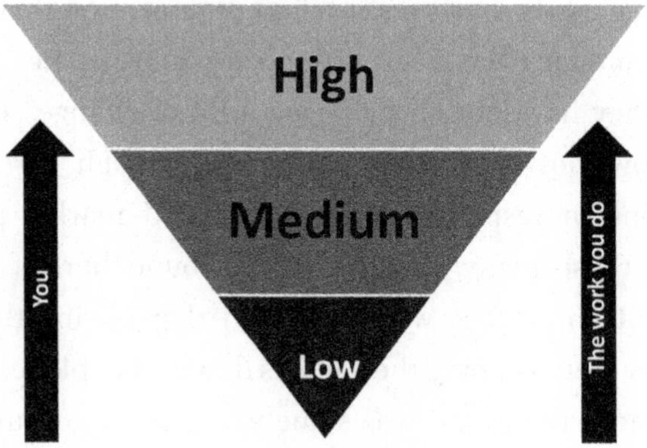

Figure 3.1

HIGH VISIBILITY

- You are **seen,** and the work that you do is **known** to your boss, colleagues in your functional area, colleagues outside of your functional area, and organizational leaders who can positively influence your career.

WHAT IS RAISING YOUR VISIBILITY?

In the *Raise Your Visibility & Value* model:

VISIBILITY IS ACTIVITIES AND BEHAVIORS THAT BUILD YOUR PRESENCE AND REPUTATION IN YOUR ORGANIZATION AND INDUSTRY.

In order to raise your visibility in your organization and industry, begin focusing on the two fundamental areas of visibility as illustrated in Figure 3.2, **presence** and **reputation.**

THE VISIBLE EMPLOYEE

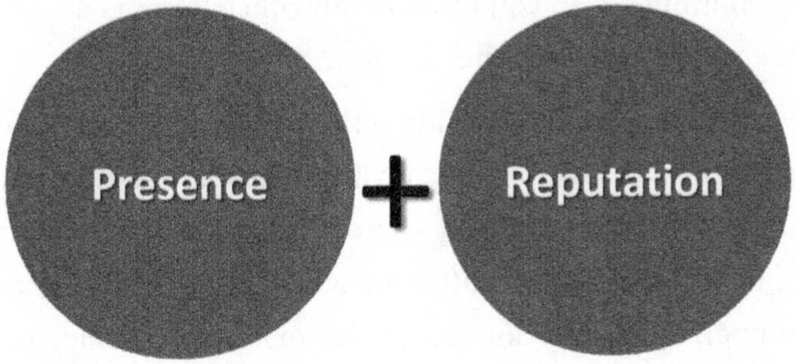

Figure 3.2

WHAT IS PRESENCE?

Presence is the *tangible* ways in which you connect with others. This is the place where activities and behaviors that help you **be seen** in your organization and industry exist. When you work to build your presence, you are seeking physical ways to connect with others as well as contribute to your organization and industry. *You cannot be visible if you are not seen by others!*

In your busy work environment, it is easy to become an office "hermit." Thousands of office hermits are spotted in corporations around the globe on a daily basis. These surreptitious creatures quietly enter their offices as dawn breaks to ensure they do not have to interact with others. While hermits' office doors are closed for most of the workday, passersby can hear the occasional sound of keys clicking on a keyboard or muffled voices on a conference call. As the sun reaches its peak, office hermits quickly dart from the confines of their offices to seek out food in a variety of places – perhaps the employee cafeteria or a local fast food restaurant. Whatever the choice, they have to be quick, as office hermits must return to their place of safety and solitude – their office – before they are seen by or have to interact with others. As the day plods on, key clicking and voice muffling continues. Then, just as at dawn, office hermits will quickly exit the building at dusk, slithering down hallways, scrunching themselves into the corners of elevators, and, with speed that would impress a jaguar on the Serengeti, depart for the day. As dawn arises the following day, the cycle continues. Can you think of any office hermits at your place of work? Are you yourself an office hermit?

Individuals successful in building their presence seize opportunities to be seen at work by "picking up their heads," getting out of their offices, and building relationships across functional areas. They identify opportunities to be seen in different ways (i.e., subject matter expert, team member, cross-functional contributor). They interact, participate, and engage with others.

WHAT IS REPUTATION?

Reputation is the *intangible* ways in which we connect with others. This is where activities and behaviors that help you **be known** in your organization and industry exist. I like to think of reputation as the echo you leave when you exit a room. Your reputation is what your colleagues say about you when you are not there. Perhaps your colleagues are commenting on a presentation you just gave, an interaction you just had, or your candidacy for a promotion. Do you know what they are saying about you? More importantly, what do you want your colleagues to be saying about you?

Similar to the office hermit situation, the global workplace is also full of office "tyrants." These troublesome creatures are very visible in their environments, just not in a good way. To survive in their fast-paced and ever-changing organizations, office tyrants feed on negative and energy-draining behavior. They create havoc while performing their job responsibilities, cause controversy on every project, and cauterize relationships in ways that impede progress. A visitor to an environment that houses an office tyrant can easily tell when the tyrant is approaching simply by watching the behavior of his colleagues. Their eyes roll, their bodies stiffen, and they often scatter for the nearest conference room or stairwell. Most troubling for office tyrants looking to create their next controversy is the fact that others are already aware of their disruptive and unproductive behavior even before meeting them. As another successful day of bad behavior comes to a close, the office tyrants withdraw, only to return the next day to feed again. Can you think of any office tyrants in your organization? Could you be an office tyrant? Do you know your reputation at work?

Individuals successful in building a good reputation are highly regarded in positive ways. Your colleagues with great reputations are not only known in positive ways by colleagues with whom they have met and collaborated, they are similarly known to colleagues whom they have yet to meet. The old adage, "your reputation precedes you," continues to exist due to individuals who are very successful in managing their reputation in their organization and industry.

How do Presence and Reputation Come Together?

Your time is precious. Your days are already packed with meetings, conference calls, overdue deliverables, and unanticipated interruptions. Working to raise your visibility in your organization and industry requires that you focus your precious time on specific activities and behaviors that help you produce results. Anyone can engage in a bevy of activities that keep them busy, yet you cannot afford that luxury. The investment of time and energy you make in your efforts to raise your visibility must be productive. What is the difference between keeping busy and being productive?

- **Keeping busy.** You engage in a number of activities that exhaust your time and energy, yet these activities do not advance your professional goals. At the end of your day, your key thought is "Where did the day go?"
- **Being productive.** You engage in specific activities in which you invest the appropriate time and energy, thus advancing your goals. At the end of your day, your key thought is "What's next?"

How do I Raise My Visibility?

As you work to raise your visibility in your organization and industry, certain activities and behaviors are more productive and will accelerate your efforts. These "accelerators" are like putting rocket fuel in a Honda Civic. When you "step on the gas," you will enhance your presence and reputation faster than ever before. And these activities and behaviors can be easily integrated into your already busy workday.

The seven **visibility accelerators** are:

1	Introduce yourself	The degree to which you introduce yourself to new colleagues and make a great first impression
2	Be accessible	The degree to which colleagues can reach you and benefit from the interaction
3	Be responsive	The degree to which you get back to your colleagues and foster progress
4	Interact with others	The degree to which you engage one-to-one with colleagues in your organization and industry
5	Participate with a purpose	The degree to which you engage in one-to-many activities with colleagues in your organization and industry
6	Engage with industry associations	The degree to which you interact and participate with colleagues *outside* of your organization
7	Manage your reputation	How your colleagues think or speak about you when you are not present

In the chapters that follow, we will take a deeper look into each of these visibility accelerators. My goal is to help you generate new insights, and provide enough information to help you build your personalized action plan to raise your visibility and value in your organization and industry.

THE VISIBILITY ACTIVITY MAP

At the end of each chapter detailing the seven visibility accelerators, you will have an opportunity to think about activities you can do to positively impact that particular behavior or strategy, and document these activities on a **visibility activity map.**

As you begin this process of building activities, keep the following suggestions in mind:

- **Keep it simple.** Start with just one or two basic activities. If you over commit and your activities are overly complex, you are less likely to make progress.

- **Keep it real.** Create activities that work for you and are realistic within your organizational culture and industry. Activities that sound good but are unlikely to become doable in your workplace will not get done.

- **Keep it going.** Your goal in creating activities is to make progress. Use the chart following each of the upcoming chapters to create an activity map - what you will do, when you will start, the risks that may exist in making progress, and how you will mitigate the risks.

HOW TO COMPLETE YOUR VISIBILITY ACTIVITY MAP

To document your thoughts and ideas for enhancing your presence in your organization and industry, utilize the following mapping tool found at the end of each chapter.

What are my activities?	How frequently will I perform this activity?	When will I start?	What is my first step?	What risk exists in making progress?	How will I address this risk?

You can download this mapping tool on the *Raise Your Visibility & Value* link at the www.excellius.com website.

Here are some tips on how to complete your grid effectively:

- **"What are my activities?"** – Identify the activities you will do to raise your visibility.
- **"How frequently will I perform this activity?"** – Identify how frequently you will do this activity.
- **"When will I start?"** – Identify how you will begin this activity.
- **"What is my first step?"** – Identify the very first step you must take to make progress.
- **"What risk exists in making progress?"** – Identify an obstacle that might impede your progress.

- **"How will I address this risk?"** – Identify what you will do to ensure the risk is merely a hurdle to overcome, not a roadblock.

VISIBILITY ACTIVITY MAP EXAMPLE

The following is an example of what an entry in your visibility activity map might look like:

What are my activities?	How frequently will I perform this activity?	When will I start?	What is my first step?	What risk exists in making progress?	How will I address this risk?
My boss is not located in the same offices as I am located, so I will meet with her to discuss my career development.	Quarterly	Q2 – May	Contact my boss by Friday to suggest this idea and gain her support.	My boss has to cancel a quarterly meeting due to a scheduling conflict.	Immediately reschedule the meeting at the earliest possible time. Ensure these meetings happen!

Chapter Three Recap

- You rationalize every day at work that being visible has no place on your to-do list and you convince yourself of the following:
  - "I do not have the time."
  - "I do not need to."
  - "It is too hard."
- Networking oftentimes is consuming, ineffective, and exhausting for employed business professionals.
- Now more than ever, being visible is critical to your long-term success.
- **Visibility** is comprised of the following two areas:
  - **Presence** is the *tangible* connection with others. Colleagues successful in building their presence interact, participate, and engage with others.
  - **Reputation** is the *intangible* connection with others. Colleagues successful in building a good reputation are thought of and spoken of in positive ways when they are not present.
- There are differences between being busy and being productive. Busy colleagues think "Where did the day go?" while productive colleagues think "What's next?"
- The seven **visibility accelerators** are:
  1. Introduce yourself
  2. Be accessible
  3. Be responsive
  4. Interact with others
  5. Participate with a purpose

6. Engage with industry associations

7. Manage your reputation

- When completing your **visibility activity map**, keep it simple, keep it real, and keep it going.

CHAPTER FOUR

Visibility Accelerator #1
Introduce Yourself

You may be surprised to read **introduce yourself** as the first *Raise Your Visibility & Value* visibility accelerator. After all, introducing yourself to others seems so simple. What is difficult about saying "hello" and shaking the hand of a new colleague?

Carl is also surprised because, like you, he has been meeting people his entire life. As an adolescent, he found himself at parties introducing himself to new friends. As a young law student, he attended classes where he introduced himself to fellow classmates. Today, as an in-house attorney for a growing software company, Carl "meets and greets" people all of the time - colleagues, clients, and other professionals in the legal profession. When you stop to think about it, Carl has met so many people in the past, you would think he could write this chapter.

Yet, regardless of the simplicity of an introduction and all of his experience, Carl is not comfortable introducing himself to others. He often avoids introducing himself, missing opportunities to meet new colleagues and raise his visibility with potential decision makers. When Carl "takes the plunge" and introduces himself, he is clumsy and uncomfortable, thus creating a poor first impression.

Like Carl, you are probably one or more of the following when you introduce yourself to a new colleague:

- **Inconsistent**. Sometimes you introduce yourself to others effectively and sometimes you do not.

- **Uncomfortable**. You find introducing yourself to be uncomfortable; you either introduce yourself quickly just to get the introduction over with or you avoid introducing yourself altogether.

- **Inattentive**. You pay little attention while you are introducing yourself – you may be shaking the hand of another, yet your mind has already moved on.

- **Underskilled**. You do not know how to introduce yourself effectively.

- **Underinvested**. You do not value the importance of a strong introduction, and you have not thought about building your skill for introducing yourself to others.

Whether you are inconsistent, inattentive, or underinvested, introducing yourself effectively is one of the foundations for raising your visibility in your organization and industry. If there is one behavior I could change that would help me feel this book is a wild success, it would be shifting your mindset regarding introducing yourself - shifting from the belief that introducing yourself is unimportant to the belief that introducing yourself is a critical behavior to embrace in today's fast-paced and frenetic organizations.

> **INTRODUCTION** IS THE DEGREE TO WHICH YOU INTRODUCE YOURSELF TO NEW COLLEAGUES AND MAKE A GREAT FIRST IMPRESSION.

WHAT HAPPENED TO THE ART OF THE INTRODUCTION?

Let's face it. At some point in the development of our society, we lost the ability to introduce ourselves to one another. I was not alive when this loss occurred, so I do not have firsthand knowledge of when this happened. I am not a sociologist, so I do not have the research skills to figure out why this occurred. I am not suggesting that our ancestors excelled at introducing themselves and that this ability mysteriously eroded over time. It does seem, however, that the attention we pay to introducing ourselves to one another peaked at some point in the past. Perhaps you can imagine the following "moments of introduction" throughout history.

Circa 1,000,000 B.C.

Grog: *"Ugga."*

Sura: *"Yug."*

Circa 1910

Gregory: *"Good afternoon. My name is Gregory Van Pelt. It is a pleasure to meet you. Lovely day, is it not?"*

Suzanne: *"Good afternoon, Mr. Van Pelt. My name is Suzanne Rockefeller. The pleasure is all mine, I am sure. It is quite the lovely day."*

Circa 2017

Greg: *"What up."*

Sue: *"Yo."*

What happened? Is it the head-spinning advances in technology, growing networks of global economies, and changing workplace demographics that we discussed in the introduction of this book? While I do not know the answer, I do know that the degradation in your ability to introduce yourself is causing you to miss an opportunity to make a strong first impression. You are more likely to say good morning to Siri than to a colleague.

John Clancy, Managing Director, Providence Equity Partners, a leading global asset company, understands the importance of a strong first impression. John has held a number of senior leadership roles throughout his career and has met hundreds of new colleagues, investors, and customers along the way. "I can't stress enough the importance of the first few seconds you have when meeting a new person. With a strong introduction, you have the opportunity to create a connection that provides you a surplus of goodwill. No one wants to start a relationship in a deficit, which takes even more effort to turn around. Making a good first impression is critical to laying a strong foundation for future interaction."

Do You or Don't You Introduce Yourself to Others?

Are you skeptical of the importance of a strong introduction? Sit back and watch the behavior of colleagues who do not know one another and do not introduce themselves at your next meeting. Discomfort reigns as it feels that something is missing. Their interactions are stilted. Progress flounders. If you are a busy business professional in an ever-evolving organization, you fall into one of the following categories when you introduce yourself to colleagues you do not know.

Avoider

You avoid introducing yourself at all costs. Perhaps you are highly uncomfortable or severely underskilled. Much like getting a flu shot, you want your introduction to be quick and painless. In fact, you would not introduce yourself to others at all if you could avoid doing so.

Do any of the following *Avoider* characteristics seem familiar to you when you think about introducing yourself to others?

- You sit down at a company meeting and immediately take out your smart phone to scroll email.

- You sit down next to a table full of colleagues at a training class and immediately look at the training material.

- You sit down at a table at a networking event and quietly "disappear" into another world, staring at anything or anyone as long as it is not someone at your table.

- You join a senior leadership meeting and you sit next to a known colleague who saved you a seat.

- You sit with a new group at a teambuilding session and *never* introduce yourself.

FUMBLER

You introduce yourself, yet you do so poorly. Perhaps you are inconsistent, inattentive, or underskilled. Perhaps you do not value the benefit of a solid introduction. Whatever the reason, your inability to introduce yourself effectively leaves others feeling unimpressed and underwhelmed.

Do any of the following *Fumbler* characteristics seem familiar to you when you think about how you introduce yourself to others?

- You take an opportunity to introduce yourself, yet you look away as you do so, reeking of disinterest.

- You only introduce yourself when a colleague starts the introduction for you.

- You are approached by a new colleague who introduces himself to you and you respond by saying "Hi," without saying your name.

- You introduce yourself to others, yet you are asked to repeat your name because you mumbled when you spoke.

- You are not focused on the colleague you are meeting, which causes you to repeatedly ask, "I'm sorry, what was your name again?"

INTRODUCER

You are consistent, attentive, skilled, and invested. You introduce yourself with energy, clarity, and confidence. You are focused on your colleague and interested in meeting him. You know that introducing yourself is an exciting opportunity to make a great first impression and a thrilling opportunity to connect with a new colleague.

Do any of the following *Introducer* characteristics seem familiar to you when you think about introducing yourself to others?

- **Energy.** You demonstrate excitement in meeting another individual. You are interested in hearing your colleague's name and any other additional information about him. Your colleagues *feel energized* simply by meeting you.

- **Confidence.** You know the importance of a good introduction and you want to create a great first impression. You express this confidence with a solid handshake (where appropriate) and a strong voice.

- **Clarity.** You know what you want to say and say it clearly and concisely.

- **Presence.** While you are introducing yourself, you are also focused on the other person. You demonstrate good eye contact and ask questions that demonstrate you are listening.

WHY DO OR DON'T YOU INTRODUCE YOURSELF TO OTHERS?

It is natural to not pay attention to something you do all the time. However, you should not confuse being *practiced* at something with being *good* at something. You eat all of the time, yet that does not mean you eat what you should. You sleep all of the time, yet that does not mean you always have a good night's sleep. Even if you have been introducing yourself to others throughout your life, you are not necessarily a world class introducer.

Your ability to introduce yourself effectively has roots in the seminal **"conscious competency"** model created by Noel Burch (Gordon Training Institute) and W. Lewis Robinson[1]. The four stages of learning suggest that you are initially unaware of how little you know about something, or unconscious of your incompetence. As recognition of your incompetence grows, you acquire a skill and begin to consciously use that skill. Eventually, you improve your effectiveness to a point of being unconsciously competent. That's our goal! You want to be naturally competent when introducing yourself to others. Let's look at an example using a growing child, Caroline, learning to tie her shoes.

- **Unconscious incompetence.** Caroline does not understand how to tie her shoes, nor does she recognize a need to do so. Subsequently, Caroline trips over her shoelaces on a recurring basis.

- **Conscious incompetence.** Tired of tripping over her dragging shoelaces, Caroline realizes that it would be helpful to tie her shoes, yet she does not know how to do so.

- **Conscious competence.** After lessons from her parents, Caroline begins to tie her own shoes, focusing on the process to tie her shoes in a step-by-step way, resulting in less tripping.

- **Unconscious competence.** Following some practice, Caroline is able to tie her shoes on her own, with very little focused attention. Tying her shoes has become second nature.

When you overlay our three introduction types – *Avoider, Fumbler,* and *Introducer* – with the four stages of learning – unconscious incompetent, conscious incompetent, conscious competent, and unconscious competent – a picture begins to emerge of one of the reasons you do or do not introduce yourself effectively, as illustrated in Figure 4.1.

INTRODUCTION MATRIX

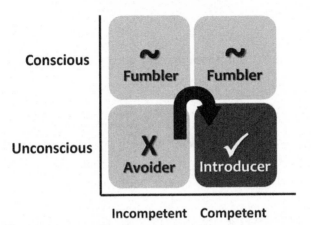

Figure 4.1

Let's use this model and watch Carl as he evolves from a fumbler to an introducer.

- **Avoider (unconscious incompetent).** Carl does not understand how to introduce himself, nor does he recognize the need to do so. He walks into a meeting, sits down, and quietly scrolls email on his smart phone.

- **Fumbler (conscious incompetent).** Tired of feeling like he is missing the benefits of introducing himself or tired of introducing himself poorly, Carl realizes it would be helpful to introduce himself effectively, yet he does not know how to do so. He is easily distracted and speaks so quickly that others don't understand him.

- **Fumbler (conscious competent).** After reading *Raise Your Visibility & Value* and learning from his *Introducer* colleagues, Carl begins to introduce himself more often, focusing on being energetic, clear, confident and present. While this takes a lot of focus, he begins to feel good about his efforts.

- **Introducer (unconscious competent).** Following a lot of practice, Carl consistently and naturally introduces himself with energy, clarity, and confidence – all while being very present in the moment.

Take a moment to think about your ability to introduce yourself to others and check one of the boxes below.

☐ I AM AN **AVOIDER** (UNCONSCIOUS INCOMPETENT). I DON'T INTRODUCE MYSELF TO OTHERS, NOR HAVE I GIVEN INTRODUCING MYSELF TO OTHERS MUCH THOUGHT.

☐ I AM A **FUMBLER** (CONSCIOUS INCOMPETENT). I KNOW THAT I NEED TO INTRODUCE MYSELF TO OTHERS, YET I DO NOT KNOW HOW TO DO SO, NOR AM I TRYING TO LEARN HOW TO INTRODUCE MYSELF MORE EFFECTIVELY.

☐ I AM A **FUMBLER** (CONSCIOUS COMPETENT). I KNOW THAT I NEED TO INTRODUCE MYSELF TO OTHERS, AND I HAVE BEEN PRACTICING ON EFFECTIVELY INTRODUCING MYSELF.

☐ I AM AN **INTRODUCER** (UNCONSCIOUS COMPETENT). I INTRODUCE MYSELF CONSISTENTLY AND DO SO WITH ENERGY, CLARITY, AND CONFIDENCE. I AM RAISING MY VISIBILITY IN MY ORGANIZATION AND INDUSTRY.

A MODEL FOR INTRODUCING YOURSELF

We have covered a lot of information in this chapter and there are a lot of labels floating around. Are you an "unconscious incompetent *Avoider*" or are you a "conscious competent *Fumbler*"? Yikes! What can frenzied business professionals in their frenetic organizations do?

Consider the following six-step model, illustrated in Figure 4.2, when working to build your confidence introducing yourself to others.

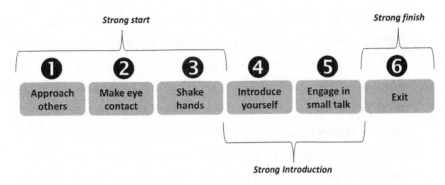

Figure 4.2

THE STRONG START

Approaching others or being receptive to the advance of others, great eye contact, and a confident handshake are key components to a **strong start**. These behaviors illustrate that you are comfortable and skilled at introducing yourself. In real time, your strong start will last from five to seven seconds. Don't underestimate, however, the difference that a few seconds can make when introducing yourself effectively.

1. **Approach Others.** Opportunities to introduce yourself will generally arrive in one of two ways - either a colleague will approach you or you will approach a colleague. Regardless of who goes first, you either need to approach new colleagues in order to introduce yourself, or be receptive to new colleagues when they approach you.

2. **Make eye contact.** Strong eye contact is one of the best ways to demonstrate that you are an attentive and invested participant. While your eye contact will vary during the conversation, focus on eye contact more when you are *listening* than when you are *speaking*. You may be the type of person who speaks visually, and in order to do so, looks away at what I call the "invisible whiteboard." This invisible whiteboard is where you do your best thinking and where you collect your thoughts in order to speak effectively. However, if you look away when your new colleague is speaking, you may appear disinterested. Maintain strong eye contact when your colleague is speaking.

3. **Shake hands.** While it might not be required or accepted in all cultures, shake hands with a new colleague when appropriate. If it does not seem to fit the moment (e.g., your colleague may not be feeling well and is not shaking hands at the moment) or there is not an opportunity to shake a new colleague's hand (e.g., your colleague's hands are full with a glass of wine and a plate of cocktail weenies), that is fine. Move on and introduce yourself. If shaking a hand of a new colleague does seem to fit the moment, give a firm but brief handshake.

THE STRONG INTRODUCTION

Your **strong introduction** is comprised of two activities:

- Introduce yourself
- Engage in small talk

A lot of networking literature refers to a concept called the "30-second commercial." This commercial is your "30 seconds of fame," an opportunity to tell new colleagues who you are and what you do.

A reminder that the focus of *Raise Your Visibility & Value* is on employed business professionals. Subsequently, you don't need to focus a lot of your attention and effort on creating, memorizing, and speaking like a commercial. When you think of commercials, you likely think of someone trying to sell you something. If fact, most of us record television programs on our Tivo recorders so we can skip the commercials! Skip the commercial and introduce yourself with simplicity and authenticity – your colleagues will appreciate it.

Most introductions also require some degree of small talk in order to avoid awkward silences. Small talk does not need to be profound or moving. If it were, we would not call it "small" talk. Small talk is designed to create a bridge between your introduction and your strong finish.

4. **Introduce yourself.** You don't need a different way of introducing yourself for every situation, so create a simple way of introducing

yourself that works most of the time. By creating a simple way of introducing yourself, you are also able to practice, build your skill set, and grow your confidence. Here are some suggestions on introductions that might work for you:

- "Hi, Kathy. Great meeting you. My name is Ed Evarts and I am a leadership coach and author."

- "Good morning. I just wanted to take an opportunity to introduce myself. My name is Ed Evarts and I am an author and leadership coach."

- "Hi. I don't think we've met. My name is Ed Evarts and I am an author and leadership coach."

A WORD ON REMEMBERING NAMES

HAVE YOU EVER NOTICED THAT THERE ARE SOME COLLEAGUES WHO SEEM TO REMEMBER NAMES BETTER THAN OTHERS? DO YOU COVET THEIR SECRET? HAVE THEY BOUGHT A DVD ON THE HOME SHOPPING NETWORK TO BUILD THEIR MEMORY SKILLS? DO THEY PICTURE A BOAT WHEN THEY MEET BOB AND A HOUSE WHEN THEY MEET HARRY?

FOR A VARIETY OF REASONS, SOME OF US ARE MORE ABLE TO REMEMBER NAMES THAN OTHERS. I DON'T KNOW THE SECRET, IF THERE REALLY IS A SECRET, OR IF THERE IS ONE SECRET THAT FITS ALL OF US. COLLEAGUES WHO SEEM TO REMEMBER NAMES, PROBABLY OUR **INTRODUCERS**, TEND TO BE ATTENTIVE AND INVESTED IN THE CONVERSATION. THEY HAVE MADE A CONSCIOUS CHOICE THAT REMEMBERING A NAME IS IMPORTANT.

INTRODUCERS REPEAT THE NAME OF THE NEW PERSON THEY JUST MET BACK TO THE PERSON AT THE POINT OF INTRODUCTION. THEY USE THE PERSON'S NAME AS THEY ENGAGE THEM IN SMALL TALK. WHEN INTRODUCING THEIR NEW COLLEAGUE TO OTHERS, **INTRODUCERS** REPEAT THEIR NEW COLLEAGUE'S NAME. WHEN YOU ARE MORE ATTENTIVE AND INVESTED, YOU WILL REMEMBER NAMES BETTER AND MORE NATURALLY.

FOR **INTRODUCERS**, REMEMBERING NAMES IS NOT A GIMMICK OR A GAME, IT IS A GOAL ON WHICH THEY ARE INTENTLY FOCUSED.

5. **Engage in small talk.** For many of you, engaging in small talk is the most painful step in this model. Similar to Senator Lloyd Bentsen's observation during the 1988 Vice Presidential debate that his opponent Dan Quayle was "no Jack Kennedy," I can assure you that I am no Emily Post. What I can tell you is that the smoothest way to create small talk is to ask questions. If you fertilize a new interaction with questions, a conversation will be born. Here are some questions you might ask a colleague you are meeting for the first time.

At your organization:

- "What do you do for (insert your company name here)?"
- "How long have you been with (insert your company name here)?"
- "What's keeping you busy these days?"
- "I don't think we've met before. How long have you been here and what do you do?"

At an industry networking event:

- "What brings you here this evening?"
- "Have you been to this event (or this location) before?"
- "Do you know many people here? Would you be kind enough to introduce me to some of your colleagues?"

THE STRONG FINISH

Regardless of how strong you started, your best efforts will be eroded without a **strong finish**. How you exit an introduction might be the last thing a new colleague remembers about you, so make sure you have a strong finish. Remember the dinner Carl, Elaine, and Susan enjoyed in Chapter 1? They were collectively "wowed" by the strong start they experienced with their waitress – she was attentive and energetic. Yet, as the dinner wore on, our diners could barely get her attention, her service diminished, and it was obvious that her only interest was in getting them their check. Do you think Carl, Elaine, and Susan left with a great impression due to their waitress's great start or a poor impression due to her weak finish?

A strong finish is also important, as a strong finish is often the first step to your next interaction with your colleague (see Chapter 7). When you connect with new colleagues, do not consider your interaction as a one-time event, but the start of a possible relationship. Strong finishes make your next strong start easier.

6. **Exit.** A key segment of a strong finish is to exit your introduction effectively. If you find yourself connecting with a colleague in ways that feel energizing and rewarding, stay with it for as long as it feels right. Conversely, staying in an introductory conversation for too long may deny you the opportunity to meet additional colleagues.

At some point, you will sense that it is time to move to another introduction. Extending an introduction long after it should have been over is not beneficial to you or your colleague. Most probably, you will extend an introduction long after it should have been over because you do not know how to end it effectively and politely. Here are some suggestions on how to exit an introduction in ways that build a bridge to your next interaction.

- "I see some other colleagues that I would like to say hello to. If you don't mind, I am going to head over to see them. Here is my business card. It has been great meeting you and I look forward to connecting again soon."

- "It has been great meeting you! Here is my business card. If you can give me your contact information, I would love to continue this conversation over coffee."

- "I'd love to continue our conversation, but I see a colleague that I need to mention something to. If you would excuse me, I am going to grab him before I miss him."

WHAT ARE *INTRODUCERS* DOING THAT CAN HELP YOU?

Introducers introduce themselves with energy, clarity, and confidence. Why reinvent the wheel? Let's take a cue from our *Introducer* colleagues and practice some of the behaviors they weave into their introductions that make Introducers so effective when connecting themselves to others. Recall that, at their best, *Introducers* are the following:

- **Consistent**. They have developed a repeatable series of steps in which they introduce themselves, similar to the model illustrated in Figure 4.2. Like the instructions on the bottle of shampoo in your shower (rinse, wash, rinse, repeat), keep it simple.

- **Attentive**. They focus on what they are doing as they introduce themselves, and they pay attention when their colleague is introducing herself. *Introducers* shake hands firmly and maintain strong eye contact.

- **Skilled**. They approach new colleagues with confidence, ask questions that create an opportunity for engaging small talk, and ensure that they exit their introduction in a strong manner.

- **Invested**. *Introducers* recognize the importance of introducing themselves in such a way as to raise their visibility in their organization and industry.

A WORD ON BEING COMFORTABLE INTRODUCING YOURSELF TO OTHERS

One other characteristic of effective *Introducers* is that they are either naturally comfortable introducing themselves to others or they have mastered the ability to diminish any short-term discomfort that arises as they introduce themselves to others.

While I believe you can build your *ability* to be consistent, attentive, skilled, and invested when introducing yourself, I think it would be presumptuous to *tell you* to be comfortable when introducing yourself.

Whether you are an *Avoider, Fumbler* or just plain unconsciously competent, some of you will not be comfortable introducing yourself, no matter how many books you read or how many times you read this book.

I believe that you can "move the dial" on your comfort level through practice and by following the suggestions shared in this chapter. I believe that when you practice, you can introduce yourself with increased energy, clarity, and confidence. I believe that as your confidence builds, your comfort level in introducing yourself to others as a way to raise your visibility in your organization will grow and even flourish.

WHAT ARE SOME WAYS YOU CAN INTRODUCE YOURSELF?

Here are some typical hurdles to introducing yourself to colleagues and suggestions for improving your introductions in your organization and industry.

Introduction Hurdles	Introduction Activities
I am not comfortable introducing myself.	• Confide in a colleague or family member that you are working to improve your ability to introduce yourself. Ask him for some suggestions and if he would practice with you. • Decide that a goal for your next meeting or event is to experiment with one or two ways to introduce yourself to others. As you are just practicing, it doesn't have to be perfect. • Take some pressure off yourself and consider using an opportunity to introduce yourself as simply a way to make a positive first impression.

I do not introduce myself to colleagues whom I do not know when attending a meeting.	• Create generic follow-up questions to use once you have introduced yourself to someone you do not know. For example:
	  • "What do you do for (insert your company name here)?"
	  • "How long have you been with (insert your company name here)?"
	  • "What's keeping you busy these days?"
	  • "I don't think we've met before. How long have you been here and what do you do here?"
	• Take a moment to introduce a new colleague to others whom you do know.
	• Repeat the name of new colleagues you have just met at a meeting in order to remember her name (e.g., *It's great meeting you, Karen.*") and use her name when introducing her to others.

Introduction Hurdles	Introduction Activities
I am not generally interested in meeting new people.	• Create incremental goals for meeting someone new. You don't have to meet everyone or be interested in meeting everyone, yet meeting new people occasionally or on your terms may be more comfortable for you. • Ask a trusted colleague to introduce you or join you when you are meeting colleagues to whom you are uncomfortable introducing yourself.
I do not actively introduce myself to colleagues I do not know when attending a social gathering hosted by my employer.	• Set a goal to introduce yourself to at least one or two colleagues whom you do not know. Social gatherings hosted by your employer are a great place to meet new colleagues. • Ask a colleague you know to attend with you and introduce yourselves in tandem. • Look for colleagues who appear to be very good at introducing themselves at a meeting. Follow-up with this colleague and ask him for tips and suggestions on how to become more proficient at introducing yourself.

MY *INTRODUCE YOURSELF* ACTIVITY GRID

What are my activities?	How frequently will I perform this activity?	When will I start?	What is my first step?	What risk exists in making progress?	How will I address this risk?

Chapter Four Recap

- **Introduction** is the degree to which you introduce yourself to new colleagues and make a great first impression. Our society has lost its ability to make effective introductions.

- You probably are one of the following when you introduce yourself to a new colleague:
  - Inconsistent
  - Uncomfortable
  - Inattentive
  - Underskilled
  - Underinvested

- Busy business professionals tend to be one of the following when it comes to introducing themselves to new colleagues:
  - Avoider
  - Fumbler
  - Introducer

- **Introducers** demonstrate the following characteristics when introducing themselves to others: **energy, confidence, clarity, and presence.**

- One reason you may not introduce yourself effectively may be reflected by where you are in the **four stages of learning**:
  - Unconscious incompetence (Avoider)
  - Conscious incompetence (Fumbler)
  - Conscious competence (Fumbler)
  - Unconscious competence (Introducer)

- A model for introducing yourself includes these steps:
  1. Approach the person
  2. Make eye contact
  3. Shake hands
  4. Introduce yourself
  5. Engage in small talk
  6. Make a strong exit

- If you are interested in remembering names, make a conscious choice to do so by being attentive and invested in the introduction conversation.

- Introducers are **consistent, attentive, skilled,** and **invested** in an introduction.

- By practicing the concepts and strategies described in this chapter, you can "move the dial" and become more comfortable introducing yourself.

- With practice comes more confidence, and with more confidence comes more comfort.

Chapter Five

Visibility Accelerator #2
Be Accessible

As a growing company in a very competitive industry, Carl's organization keeps him very busy. To stay ahead of this unending volume of work, Carl hides in his office. He spends the day dodging colleagues, letting his phone go unanswered, and surfing his inbox to select which emails are the most urgent. Carl's colleagues feel frustrated that they cannot get his attention; and on those rare occasions when they do, they feel rushed. Carl is inaccessible to colleagues who need his help and attention. He is slowly losing contact with individuals who are important to his career. His relevance in the organization is fading.

Being **accessible** is not just having an "open door policy" or ensuring your team knows your cell phone number. Accessibility is about creating an atmosphere where your colleagues can reach you – even interrupt you – and leave the interaction with a positive feeling.

> **ACCESSIBILITY** IS THE DEGREE TO WHICH COLLEAGUES CAN REACH YOU AND BENEFIT FROM THE INTERACTION.

Are you accessible? Perhaps you possess low self-awareness of how your behavior in your organization diminishes outreaches by others. You can be heard decrying, "No one ever tells me anything!" and "How come I am always the last to hear about these things?" When you think about it, you may discover that you are less accessible than you think you are. Do any of the following characteristics seem familiar to you when you think about being accessible to others?

- Your office door is always closed.
- You rush frantically between conference calls or meetings with little time to talk to others.
- You easily get annoyed when colleagues reach out to you (especially if the outreach feels like an interruption).
- Your back faces the entrance to your office or workstation.
- Your interactions with your colleagues never seem to benefit them.
- No one comes to you for help.

WHAT ARE THE BENEFITS OF BEING ACCESSIBLE?

Being accessible benefits everyone. Ram Reddy is the Chief Information Officer at The Rockport Group, offering high-quality dress and casual footwear to customers globally. Despite the daily challenges he faces in his busy workplace, Ram is committed to being accessible to those who reach out to him. "Being accessible is a key part of collaboration. Although many of us have offices that physically separate us from one another, it is important to act as though there are no walls. If a colleague needs me, I want her to be able to get to me. Likewise, I like getting out of my office and, rather than email a colleague a question, ask her my question or follow-up with her in person. This also allows my colleague to access me in ways that help her."

When you work to be accessible to your colleagues, you are the one who truly benefits, because you:

- **Identify issues and problems early**, leading to quicker resolution, enhanced productivity, and reduced frustration.
- **Increase your influence** in your organization as you become a "go-to" person who is known for helping others solve problems.

- **Create opportunities** for you to participate in activities that are meaningful to your career and organization.

- **Bolster your reputation** in your organization and industry by modeling behavior that your colleagues can emulate.

WHAT IS THE DIFFERENCE BETWEEN TANGIBLE AND INTANGIBLE ACCESSIBILITY?

As we reviewed in Chapter 3, visibility is comprised of presence (the tangible ways that individuals connect with you) and reputation (the intangible ways that individuals connect with you). Similarly, accessibility has tangible and intangible characteristics.

TANGIBLE ACCESSIBILITY

- **Ensure your colleagues know where your office or workstation is located.** Some corporate offices are labyrinths and finding your office may not be as easy as it sounds. Concurrently, some corporate offices have "cubicle farms" – dozens and dozens of similarly looking workstations that abut one another. Your colleagues could go insane trying to find your location. Rather than confirming that mental health is covered under your organization's insurance plan, make sure that your colleagues know where your office or workstation is located.

- **Ensure your colleagues know the hours that you work.** In today's busy and fast-paced organizations, you may have non-standard schedules, either to fit the needs of the business or to respond to personal needs. You may work Tuesday through Saturday, or work a half-day on Wednesdays, or take Fridays off. Regardless of your schedule, make sure that your colleagues know your days and hours of work.

- **Ensure your colleagues know your contact information.** Sometimes your colleagues are unable to access you because they simply do not have your email address, office phone number extension, or cell phone number. Many corporate switchboards are now automated and if your colleagues do not know your extension number or how to spell your name in the "dial-by-name" directory, finding you can become frustrating. Make sure that your colleagues have your contact information for easy access to you. One easy way is to include your office and cell phone numbers in your email signature.

- **Ensure your colleagues know when you are *not* accessible.** As important as it is to create access, it is equally important to ensure that your colleagues know when you are not accessible. You may be out of the office at a meeting, traveling, ill, or, on a rare occasion, enjoying a personal day. Make sure that your colleagues know when you are not available, whom they can contact during your absence, and when you will return to your office. For example, you can create the following "out-of-office" email that your colleagues will automatically receive until you are back in the office.

"I am currently out of the office, returning next Thursday, July 22nd. If your need is urgent, please contact Susan Jones at 555-555-5555. If you are able to wait, I will begin returning emails when I return to the office. Thank you in advance for your patience."

INTANGIBLE ACCESSIBILITY

Your reputation is based on the intangible ways that folks connect with you.

- **Do you create a welcoming atmosphere that reflects your desire to be accessible?** When your colleagues come to see you, is your behavior creating or hindering access? Here are some ways to create a welcoming atmosphere that inspires access:

  - **Place your office or workstation chair facing the door.** This way, you are able to see colleagues as they enter your office or workstation. When your back is facing the entrance to your office or workstation, you subliminally are sending the message, "Don't interrupt me."

- **Stand and welcome colleagues to your office or workstation.** To minimize the perception that they are interrupting you, demonstrate that your colleagues are not bothering you by physically welcoming them to the conversation.

- **Ask your colleagues how you can help them.** Even though your colleagues have come to see you, take the lead. When you answer your phone, you are the first one to say something like "Hi. This is Carl." When you respond to a knock on your door, you are the first one to say something like "Hello. Can I help you?" Colleagues entering your office or workstation should be treated in the same way. Welcome colleagues to your office by taking the first step.

- **Sit next to your colleagues, not behind your desk.** One of the best ways to be accessible is to get out from behind your desk and sit next to colleagues. This may reduce any unintended positions of power and will create better conversations.

- **Do your interactions with colleagues inspire them to reach out to you again?** Once you have welcomed your colleagues into the conversation, is your behavior helping or hindering the reason your colleagues came to see you in the first place? Although we will talk about *Being Responsive* in more detail in the next chapter, here are some ways to inspire your colleagues to reach out to you in the future:

  - **Have the answer at that moment.** This is the simplest way to ensure that your colleagues benefit from their interaction with you. You have an answer to their need and you can provide the answer at that moment.

- **Have the answer, yet you are not available at the moment.** Just because someone is attempting to ask you a question or ask for help does not mean you have to respond at that moment. Your fast-paced and frenzied work organizations do not leave a lot of free time for unanticipated interruptions. If you are not available at the moment colleagues comes to see you, yet you can help them, let your colleagues know that you are busy at the moment and schedule a time to reconnect.

- **You don't have an answer, yet promise to get an answer for them.** You may be the best person to help your colleagues, yet you don't know the answer. Let your colleagues know you can help them but you will need time to get the answer, and schedule a time to reconnect.

- **Direct them to someone who may have an answer when you don't.** You don't have to know everything! If you are not the best person to help your colleagues, don't just send them away without benefiting from their interaction with you. Identify another colleague who can assist them further.

What is the Relationship between Accessibility and the Benefits Your Colleagues Receive?

It is not enough that you are highly accessible to your colleagues; your colleagues must also benefit from the interaction. After all, what is the point of being highly accessible if the interaction does not benefit your colleagues? Why would your colleagues reach out to you in the first place if not to obtain a benefit from the interaction? Take a look at the types of accessibility illustrated in Figure 5.1 to help you visualize the relationship between access and benefit.

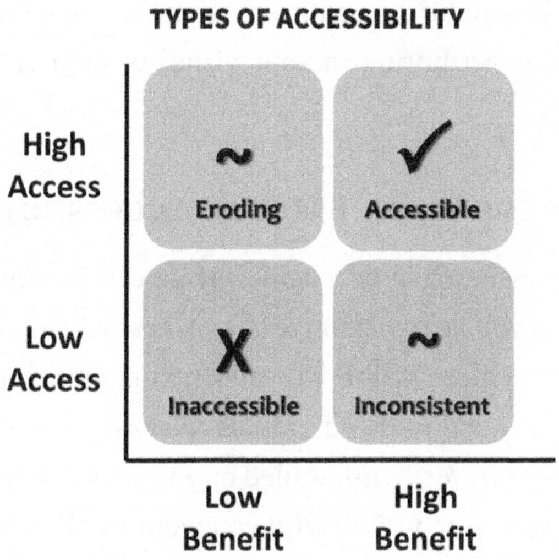

TYPES OF ACCESSIBILITY

Figure 5.1

- **Low Access + Low Benefit.** Due to your behavior, you are at risk of being **inaccessible** to colleagues in your organization and industry. In many ways, you are creating a self-fulfilling prophecy – you are not accessible to colleagues and, at that rare moment that they gain access to you, your colleagues do not benefit from the interaction.

- **Low Access + High Benefit.** While your colleagues benefit from their interactions with you, their ability to gain access to you is **inconsistent.** You are at risk of creating frustration on the part of your colleagues, which may lead to them to go elsewhere. It is common for colleagues to say to one another, "She's a great resource if you can get to her."

- **High Access + Low Benefit.** You have created a strong environment of access for your colleagues. However, your colleagues are not benefiting from their interactions with you, **eroding** their interest in coming to see you. You are at risk of being viewed as irrelevant.

- **High Access + High Benefit.** You are demonstrating the right behavior for your colleagues to access you and feel that the interaction is benefiting them. Your high level of being **accessible** is positively contributing to your visibility in your organization and industry.

WHAT HAPPENS WHEN I MODEL ACCESSIBILITY?

Think of being accessible as a two-way street. Imagine if the key leaders with whom you are working to gain access were not accessible – your great plan to be more visible in your organization would instantly crumble. Similarly, imagine if individuals who were working to raise their visibility with you were stonewalled by your inaccessible behavior – their great plan to be more visible with you would stall before it started. By being accessible, as illustrated in Figure 5.2, you are demonstrating the behavior to others that you yourself are looking to receive from others. More and more of your colleagues will emulate your behavior and increase their accessibility. Consequently, you enhance your ability to gain access to colleagues and benefit from those interactions.

SELF-FULFILLING ACCESSIBILITY

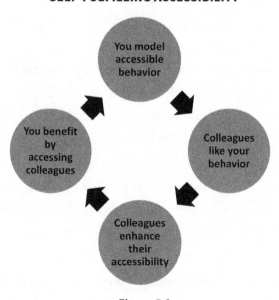

Figure 5.2

A Caveat Emptor on Being Accessible

Accessibility does not mean you are available 24/7/52. We all have limits on the degree to which we can be reached by co-workers, and you should feel comfortable enforcing and expecting others to honor these limits.

Can you be so successful modeling accessible behavior that too many colleagues want a moment of your time and you find that you have no time for yourself? Is this an example of "too much of a good thing"? We all know that sunlight is a good thing, yet too much can cause skin cancer. We know that the human body needs sugar to survive, and yet too much may cause diabetes. If you are wildly successful at being accessible, you may find your calendar and productivity under attack.

Your goal is to make sure you are being accessible to serve the needs of others, not to become a servant to accessibility. Individuals successful at being accessible also demonstrate some of the following behaviors:

- For advance requests to see you, schedule times that work within your calendar.

- For unexpected knocks on your office door, ask if the question/ topic is urgent or not. If not urgent, say something like the following:

   "I'm interested in speaking with you, yet I have a report that I am working on that is due in about an hour. Can we schedule a time for us to chat? Let's quickly look at our calendars and schedule something."

- For topics that are urgent for which you do not have time to address, ensure that your unexpected visitor knows that you have only a moment of time. Focus your comments on next steps and possibly identifying another individual who can act on your behalf.

   "I'm interested in speaking with you, yet I have a report that I am working on that is due in about an hour. Can you give me a one-

minute recap of the situation so I can at least help you identify your next step?"

- For times when you need to focus on work without interruption, find an available conference room, a vacant office, or the employee cafeteria. Seek other ways to get your work done before you stay in your office and close your door.

A WORD ON ACCESSIBILITY AND RESPONSIVENESS

Chapter 6 is focused on being responsive. It is important to note that accessibility and responsiveness are like a revolving door. If you are accessible, your colleagues will come to you with information, questions, and challenges. If you are being responsive, your colleagues' challenges will be solved and their questions answered. For the door to revolve effectively, accessibility and responsiveness must always be in play and in balance.

WHAT ARE SOME WAYS YOU CAN BE ACCESSIBLE?

Here are some typical hurdles to accessibility and suggestions for improving your accessibility in your organization and industry.

Accessibility Hurdles	Accessibility Activities
I am generally at my desk more than I am away from my desk.	• Find colleagues who seem to have figured it out. Talk with them about how they spend their time and brainstorm on ways that you can get out of your office or workstation more. • Schedule time each workday or on a frequently recurring basis to get out of your office or workstation. • Look for opportunities to do certain work elsewhere in your office area or building. All of your work does not have to be done in your office or workstation. • Meet a colleague in her office or a common area (i.e., employee cafeteria) when she asks to meet with you.
If I have an office, my door is likely closed.	• Leave your office door open all the time and assess the impact. Start small - do this for a day, and then two days, and then a week. • Consider doing some of your work away from your office so that the door is open more. Schedule time to use a conference room to get some of your work done. This way, at least your door is not closed. • Schedule times when you need to close your door so that your colleague knows when they can see you. For example, conduct your "closed door" work between 10:00am and noon or 3:00pm and 5:00pm.
I don't feel I help my colleagues as much as I would like when I meet with them.	• Confirm the goals of an upcoming meeting with a colleague and the outcomes your colleague needs in order to make progress. • Ask your colleague, at the start of the conversation, to confirm the outcomes he needs in order to make progress. • Pause and confirm with your colleague that the conversation is helping her make progress. If the conversation is not helping her make progress, ask her to restate her goals and outcomes so you can get the conversation back on track. • Ask your colleague if the conversation was helpful as the conversation comes to a close. If your colleague does not respond in a positive way, ask how else you can help him make progress.
I have my back to colleagues when they enter my office/ workstation.	• Ask your office services team to reconfigure your workspace to improve accessibility. • Put a sign at the opening of your workstation inviting visitors to knock so that you are aware of their presence.

MY *BE ACCESSIBLE* ACTIVITY GRID

What are my activities?	How frequently will I perform this activity?	When will I start?	What is my first step?	What risk exists in making progress?	How will I address this risk?

Chapter Five Recap

- **Accessibility** is the degree to which colleagues can reach you and benefit from the interaction.

- Accessibility is about creating an atmosphere where your colleagues feel they can reach you – even interrupt you – and leave the interaction with a positive feeling.

- The benefits of being accessible include your ability to:

  - Identify issues and problems early

  - Increase your influence

  - Create opportunities

- You create accessibility when you ensure colleagues know:

  - Where your office or workstation is located

  - The hours that you work

  - Your contact information

  - When you are available

- You also create accessibility when:

  - Your colleagues feel welcomed

  - Your colleagues feel inspired to reach out to you again in the future

- By modeling accessible behavior, you enhance your ability to access others and you raise your visibility in your organization and industry.

- Ensure that you manage your accessibility to minimize impact to your personal productivity. Your goal is to ensure you are being accessible to serve the needs of others, not become a servant to accessibility.

Chapter Six

Visibility Accelerator #3
Be Responsive

Even to the casual observer, there is little doubt that Carl is a busy individual. He has piles of work to complete, dozens of meetings to attend, numerous conference calls to join, and endless emails to answer. When Carl eventually leaves the office, it is highly likely that multiple emails sit unanswered in his inbox and many voice messages rest unheard on his phone. Carl wants to get back to his colleagues, yet he struggles to do so.

As recently as the early 1990's, the only way you could contact a colleague (other than visit her in person) was to call her office phone, which was hardwired to a wall next to her desk. Important documents were sent via the United States mail, an interoffice envelope, or a fax machine. If your colleague was out of her office, there was no way to contact her until she returned and either listened to your voicemail, opened the interoffice envelope or read your fax. Can you imagine? Seriously - sit, close your eyes, and visualize this type of communication environment. Even for those of us who experienced it, it is hard to believe we operated like that.

During this primitive period, response times were longer for two reasons:

1. You generally could only be reached during work hours (unless colleagues, clients, or vendors called you at home, which was unlikely).

2. Information took longer to get to you.

Today, colleagues and information can reach you at any time of the day, in an endless number of ways, in milliseconds. It is estimated that over 6 billion mobile phone calls are made per day in the United States.[1] Smartphones have created a world of socially acceptable stalking. You can be found at anytime and anywhere.

This ability to connect to you frequently and instantly highlights an interesting human behavior. The speed in which a colleague reaches you creates an identical expectation as to how long it will take you to respond. Similar to a fast-paced ping pong game, your colleagues expect a response as quickly as they got the ball to your side of the table. If this behavior was a math equation, it might look like this:

SRch (speed of reach) = SRsp (speed of response)

A colleague just sent you a text - why haven't you responded? A colleague just left you a voicemail - why haven't you called back? Even the most diligent and well-meaning business professional will stumble in his efforts to get back to everyone in a timely fashion.

Your colleagues also do not have a lot of time – their world is as frenetic as yours. When your colleagues do reach you, they need your help in order to keep moving forward.

> **RESPONSIVENESS** IS THE DEGREE TO WHICH YOU GET BACK TO COLLEAGUES AND FOSTER PROGRESS.

Have you been labeled as unresponsive? Do your colleagues use the phrases "black hole," "bottomless pit" or "it's like pulling teeth" when describing the challenges in reaching you? Your colleagues are reaching out to you for a reason. Most of the time, your colleagues are contacting you to obtain something from you (i.e., information, an opinion) in order to make progress on whatever is important to them. Some colleagues may be reaching out just to say "hello," yet even those colleagues are looking for something – opportunities to build a professional relationship with you. If you have been labeled as a "black hole," you are injuring your visibility in two ways:

- Your unresponsiveness impacts negatively on the progress of others.

- Your unresponsiveness impacts the desire for others who might want to reach out to you in the future.

These behaviors are visibility decelerators – your unresponsiveness creates frustration and damages relationships. You become an obstructionist of individual and organizational progress.

Do any of the following characteristics seem familiar to you when you think about being responsive to others?

- You _never_ return phone calls or respond to your email.

- You have to be caught "live" in your office or on the phone in order for your colleague to connect with you.

- You don't recognize (and in some cases, don't care) that you are unresponsive.

- When you do get back to your colleagues, you mask your behavior with self-effacing humor or by overusing happy face emoticons. For example, "I totally forgot to get back to you on this! Another topic for my therapist and me...! Anyway, still working on it..."

Being responsive is not about always getting back to everyone instantly. To paraphrase Abraham Lincoln, "You can get back to some of your colleagues all of the time, and all of your colleagues some of the time, but you cannot get back to all of your colleagues all of the time."

WHAT IS MY RESPONSIVENESS GOAL?

The first question you might ask yourself is "Should I aspire to be 100% responsive?" In reality, being able to respond to every incoming email, phone call (office and cell), and in-person outreach by colleagues is impossible. In 2015, the average number of emails received per day by a corporate employee was 84. (I know. I know. It feels like so much more!) In an 8-hour workday, this is approximately 10 emails per hour or one email every 6 minutes! And this is just an average – most of my clients report receiving hundreds of emails per day. Add on numerous incoming phone calls and multiple impromptu hallway conversations and it is easy to see that responding to all of your colleagues all of the time is not realistic.

Consider the relationship between the volume of outreaches you experience in a day and the time it takes to respond to them. It is safe to assume that during a fixed workday, as the number of outreaches to you increases, the time you have to respond to each outreach becomes compressed, and your response time slows, as illustrated in Figure 6.1.

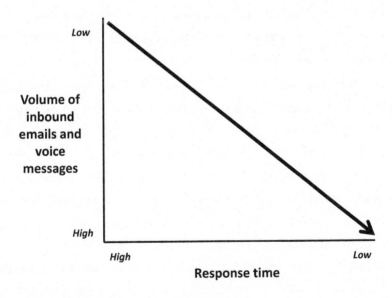

Figure 6.1

Since you cannot control the number of inbound outreaches to you, it is hard to create a goal that you will be 100% responsive. Interestingly, individuals attempting to be 100% responsive may find themselves getting little else done – potentially ignoring other areas at work that are more important to themselves, their colleagues, and their organization.

What can you do? You can enhance your *degree* of responsiveness. Even a small increase in the speed or frequency of your responsiveness will have a huge impact.

How Can I Enhance My Degree of Responsiveness?

You may feel that you should not respond to colleagues until you have the answer to their questions or requests. You may assume that others know you are working on their problem and you don't feel a need to keep them updated. You may rationalize that you are too busy to get back to anyone except your boss. While these are reasonable perspectives, days could go by before you have an answer (especially if you are dependent on others for information) and colleagues who originally reached out to you may feel forgotten. Without a response or an update, your colleagues are unsure if you received their email or if you are working on their request at all, allowing frustration to grow and progress to stall.

Harry Ebbighausen, a retired president from Iron Mountain Incorporated, the world's largest records management company, has mastered the ability to be highly responsive. Despite his voluminous workload and hectic travel schedule supporting a $3 billion enterprise, Harry possesses a reputation throughout Iron Mountain and the records management industry as a person who "gets back to everyone," whether the individual reaching out to him is a fellow executive or a truck driver at a distant facility. Harry's reason for being responsive is clear. "It's a matter of respect," says Harry. "If a colleague or an employee is taking the time to reach out to you, there must be a good reason. You demonstrate respect to others by responding to their outreach as quickly as you can." At the same time, "if you don't respond to others quickly, they will either not reach out to you again or fill-in their own answer to their problems. Sometimes, it may not be a good answer."

To enhance your degree of responsiveness, reduce frustration, improve relationships, and accelerate organizational progress, utilize the model illustrated in Figure 6.2 to ensure you are not a "bottomless pit."

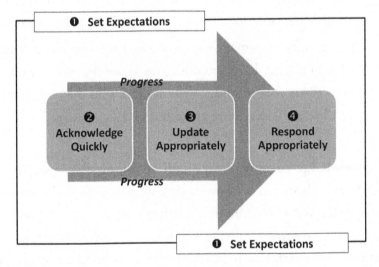

Figure 6.2

Set expectations. Although you cannot control the number of inbound outreaches to you, you can set expectations regarding how your colleagues will hear back from you. Expectations are the boundaries you create which reflect your unique style, calendar and workload. Here are some ways to set expectations/boundaries with your colleagues:

- Establish, communicate, and honor a 24-hour response rule where you say in your emails and voicemails that you will respond to your colleagues within 24 hours of your receipt of their outreach. It is generally understood that this means Monday if the message is left from Friday to Sunday.

- Schedule specific time on your calendar to respond to voicemails and emails.

- Utilize the "out-of-office" functionality embedded in your email system when you know you will be unable to access email or voicemail (i.e., you are attending a three-day off-site meeting or you are on vacation), and ensure you include the following:

  - Date and/or time you will be returning to the office.

  - The name, title, phone number, and email address of an individual your colleagues can reach during your absence.

- Update your voicemail every time you are out for an extended period of time to let your colleagues know that you are out of the office, when you will be returning, and who they can contact in your absence if they have an urgent need.

Acknowledge receipt of an email or phone message. There is a big difference between acknowledging an outreach and providing an answer to the outreach. You may not have the answer or you may not have the time to provide the answer at that moment. Regardless of the situation and in order to help your colleagues make progress, you do need to acknowledge your colleagues. By acknowledging receipt of an email or a phone message, you will benefit in the following ways:

- You ensure that your colleagues know that you received the message, reducing the likelihood that your colleagues will send another email looking for an update, or call again to confirm that you received the message in the first place.

- You are able to set new expectations that reflect your calendar and workload.

- You reduce some of the frustration that your colleagues may experience as time passes without a response.

What does "quickly" mean? Regardless of whether it was Plato or Shakespeare who popularized the often quoted "Beauty is in the eye of the beholder," quickness is also in the eye of the beholder. Attempting to meet all of your colleagues' expectations for quickness is as unlikely as all of your colleagues thinking the outfit you have on today looks "fantastic!" Your goal is to set an expectation that you can follow consistently, so that your colleagues know what to expect from you.

If you can't commit to the "24-hour rule" (don't commit to something you cannot fulfill), the next best strategy to set response time expectations is the "24/48/72" model. Regardless of the number of daily outreaches you receive, you should respond to the majority of colleagues within 24 hours, and you should have contacted the vast majority of them within 72 hours, as illustrated in Figure 6.3. This does not mean all of the topics have been resolved. This means you have contacted them in order to keep things moving.

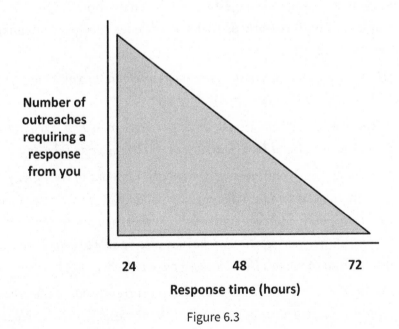

Figure 6.3

Another strategy for you to consider suggests that not all outreaches to you have to be responded to in the manner they were received. Assuming you are double-booked, time-restricted, and struggling to get your own work done, use the activities identified in the following chart to enhance your responsiveness:

Type of Outreach to You	Acknowledgment Activity
Email	Email
Phone call message	**Email** (If you call back, you are at risk of beginning an extended conversation that your calendar cannot afford)
Live phone call or office visit	Handle in the moment or reschedule in the moment

When you are using the suggestions in the chart shown above, here are examples of **email responses** that acknowledge receipt of an email or a phone message:

- *"Hi, Tom. Just a quick note that I got your email (or voice message) and I will get back to you by Wednesday."*

- *"Hi, Mary. Thank you for your email (or voice message). I will have time to review it and I will get back to you by the end of the day."*

- *"Hi, Steve. I got your message (or email). I am out of the office for the next two days and I will get you an update by next Tuesday the 20th. If this does not meet your needs, please reach out to Amir (ext. 1234), or Francine (ext. 4321), who may also be able to help. If you do reach out to someone else, please keep me posted."*

- Automated out-of-office message: *"I am currently out of the office, returning next Thursday the 22nd. If your need is urgent, please contact Susan Jones at 555-555-5555, or sjones@response.com. If you are able to wait, I will begin returning emails when I return to the office. Thank you in advance for your patience."*

Update appropriately. Once you have quickly acknowledged your colleagues' outreach, you need to keep them updated on the status of their outreach. You may not have started working on it yet or you have been working on it and you don't have a response yet. By keeping your colleagues updated, you will benefit in the following ways:

- You continue to manage expectations that reflect your calendar and workload.

- You continue to reduce some of the frustration that your colleagues may experience as time passes without a next step or conclusion.

- You provide your colleagues the information and opportunity to change how they are working to satisfy their outreach. For example, your colleagues may decide to speak to someone else to get a resolution.

Respond appropriately. At some point, you will either have the answer your colleagues need or realize that you do not. If you have the answer they need – great! However, once you know that you are unable to help, let your colleagues know as soon as possible so they can go elsewhere. Avoid becoming the "black hole" or "bottomless pit" that exists in so many organizations - respond no matter what. In order to help your colleagues make progress, consider the following messages:

- *"I've tried to figure out what is wrong with the spreadsheet you asked me to look at and I cannot find the problem. Rather than keep you waiting any longer, I think you should call Frederick in Accounts Payable who knows more about these types of spreadsheets than I do. His extension is 455."*

- *"I gave this my best shot and I still can't figure it out. Have you thought about going back to the client for more information?"*

- *"I was able to make some progress. I forwarded this to Debbie Smith in Marketing and asked her if she could help us."*

THE VOLUME FALLACY

Not all who are unresponsive can blame the overwhelming amount of incoming emails and phone calls as the cause of their behavior. Many of us tend to assume that other people's low responsiveness is due to workload when, in reality, they may not possess a natural predilection to getting back to others in a timely fashion, if at all. Consider the various places you could find yourself when you attempt to balance a desire to be responsive with your actual responsiveness, as illustrated in Figure 6.4.

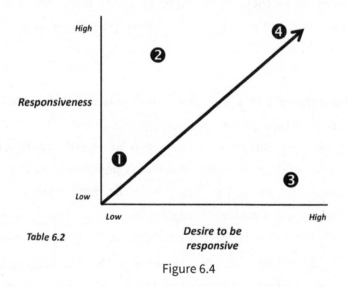

Table 6.2

Figure 6.4

1. **Low desire to be responsive + low responsiveness.** You are not very responsive, as you have little to no interest in responding to others. You are at risk of being seen as an obstructionist to progress, and your colleagues are going to simply exclude you

and work around you. Your relevance in your organization is in jeopardy.

2. **Low desire to be responsive + high responsiveness.** You are likely in a role where external factors (not personal desires) require you to be responsive. These types of roles may include, for example, a call center representative or a customer service specialist. You may find yourself in performance jeopardy as this role does not suit you well.

3. **High desire to be responsive + low responsiveness.** You represent the vast majority of busy business professionals. You really want to get back to your colleagues in a timely fashion, yet your workday is over before you have a chance to do so. The frustration your colleagues are experiencing is exceeded only by your own frustration.

4. **High desire to be responsive + high responsiveness.** You are making a difference in your organization by supporting your colleagues. You successfully satisfy your innate desire to be responsive in a timely manner, and thus reduce stress and enable progress.

Being responsive is one of the hardest challenges facing busy professionals in today's workplaces. The endless onslaught of incoming requests, calls, emails, and texts is unprecedented in human history. At the same time, being responsive is one of the strongest ways to raise your visibility in your organization. Remember that you don't have to be 100% responsive. Your personal success rests with you being *more responsive* than you currently are.

WHAT ARE SOME WAYS YOU CAN BE RESPONSIVE?

Here are some typical hurdles to responsiveness and suggestions for improving your responsiveness in your organization and industry.

Responsiveness Hurdles	Responsiveness Activities
I do not respond quickly to colleagues who contact me for help.	• Create a "first in, first out" log to ensure you get back to your colleagues faster and in the order of their outreaches to you. • Respond quickly to your colleagues to let them know that you are working on his request and your anticipated day of completion. By setting expectations you eliminate unnecessary follow-up email and phone calls. • Investigate if your e-mail management system allows you to color code email from certain colleagues. This way, you can prioritize your responses. • Work to respond to voicemail and email within twenty-four hours. • Update your voicemail and email auto responder to reflect when you will be delayed in your response time. Upon realizing you are not available, some colleagues may seek their answers elsewhere, thus reducing your workload. • Consider sending an email in response to a voicemail. While human interaction is always preferable, a quick acknowledgment is better than no acknowledgment at all.
I do not update colleagues when my efforts to respond takes longer than expected.	• Call your colleagues as soon as possible to discuss a new deadline. • Leave your colleagues a message if you are unable to connect with them live, to ensure they have their information as early as possible. • Consider alternatives to meeting the deadline that may include the assistance of other colleagues.
I do not feel I have time to get back to everyone.	• Schedule some daily time on your calendar dedicated to returning phone calls and email. • Ask your colleagues when they will need an answer. It is often not as quickly as you might think. • Read the *Harvard Business Review* article, Manage Your Energy, Not Your Time, by Tony Schwartz and Catherine McCarthy (October 2007).

MY *BE RESPONSIVE* ACTIVITY GRID

What are my activities?	How frequently will I perform this activity?	When will I start?	What is my first step?	What risk exists in making progress?	How will I address this risk?

Chapter Six Recap

- **Responsiveness** is the degree to which you get back to colleagues and foster progress.

- Being responsive is about creating an atmosphere where you get back to your colleagues in ways that eliminate becoming a "black hole."

- Your goal is not to be 100% responsive. Your goal is to *enhance* your degree of responsiveness.

- To enhance your degree of responsiveness:
  - Set expectations
  - Acknowledge quickly
  - Update appropriately
  - Respond appropriately

- Expectations are the boundaries you create for being responsive, which reflect your style, calendar and workload.

- "Quickly" is a measurement that is in the eye of the beholder. It is impossible to satisfy everyone, so use the "24/48/72-hour" rule to manage your acknowledgments.

- Updating your colleagues on the status of your progress is critical to continue to manage expectations and ensure progress.

- It's not all about volume! You may not possess a natural predilection to be responsive. Identify your natural tendencies and understand the professional risks you create for yourself.

Chapter Seven

Visibility Accelerator #4
Interact with Others

Remember the office hermits described earlier? These are the colleagues who, hidden within the confines of their offices or workstations, click away on their computer keyboards, mumble their way through conference calls behind closed doors, and slip in and out of their offices and workstations as quickly and silently as they can. It is almost as if they are members in a secret society comprised of individuals that pride themselves on *how few colleagues* they interact with on a daily basis.

If you are an office hermit, you are at risk of being just a body in a chair or a voice on the phone. When working to raise your visibility in your organization and industry, you must interact with colleagues.

> **INTERACTING** IS THE DEGREE TO WHICH YOU ENGAGE ONE-TO-ONE WITH COLLEAGUES IN YOUR ORGANIZATION AND INDUSTRY.

You may not realize that you are at risk of becoming an office hermit, even if you feel as though you are interacting with a lot of colleagues. When you take a moment to step back and look at with whom you are interacting and how frequently you are interacting, you may find that:

- You are interacting with the same three or four colleagues.

- You are interacting with individuals who are not key decision makers and influencers.

- You are not interacting as much as you think you are.

When I describe the degree to which you engage one-to-one with colleagues in your organization and industry, I am not describing free time, down time, or unproductive time. In the *Raise Your Visibility & Value* model, interacting is not about adding activities to your already overbooked workday. After all, it is unlikely that you will participate in activities that you need to add to your workday if you are already overbooked and overwhelmed.

In contrast, the interactions created when you work to raise your visibility are already part of your workday. So, why are you not engaging in these interactions? Perhaps you are not noticing these opportunities. Perhaps you are not taking advantage of them. Perhaps your organization's culture does not support them.

Or, maybe you think or have been told that the only way to raise your visibility is to network. Most of your colleagues tell you that the primary strategy to "get ahead" is to network and that you need to do so a lot. Remember that this is true for individuals looking for a job and those who are self-employed. In the *Raise Your Visibility & Value* model, for employed business professionals, networking is simply *one of many* interaction activities in which you can engage.

THE BENEFITS OF INTERACTING WITH OTHERS

As you work to expand your interactions beyond networking, you should consider the benefits of increasing the degree to which you interact with others. By interacting with colleagues at your organization, you

- **Increase your knowledge** of what is occurring at your fast-paced organization, which will position you to ride the wave of change instead of being surprised and adversely impacted by change.
- **Build clearer opinions** as to the competencies and capabilities of your colleagues as well as your organization's direction.

- **Increase your productivity** by utilizing the information gained from your increased knowledge about the business and your colleagues.

- **Influence decisions** that your colleagues are considering by sharing information, opinions, and thoughts.

NATURE OR NURTURE?

While Carl may view himself as sociable and likeable, he may not see that the demands of his organization are preventing him from interacting with others. He wants to have lunch with colleagues. He wants to spend some time with new co-workers to share "the ropes" with them. He would love to get to know individuals outside of his close-knit legal team – maybe those colleagues in marketing or engineering, for example. After all, he does work for a software technology company – perhaps these colleagues could help him understand the company's product line and its customer base better. Yet, day after day and month after month, Carl neglects to do these things. He rarely has lunch with a colleague. New team members bobble along, finding their own way, and the depth of his relationship with those individuals in Marketing and Engineering is reflected in a quick smile or glance as they pass each other in the hallway. Sometimes he feels as if he has a split personality – the friendly, easy-going individual he is at home versus the isolated, heads-down contributor he is at work. What happens to Carl once he walks into his office building?

Or, perhaps Carl is not interested in interacting with others at work at all. While he is generally a sociable and likeable fellow with his friends and family, he has little interest in spending time with colleagues at work. It is not because Carl does not like his colleagues. He just views this time as unproductive. Carl's company is growing by leaps and bounds. In order to survive in a competitive market place and his fast-paced and changing work organization, who has time for lunch with colleagues? After all, lunch is a great time to get some work done. Who has time to help new colleagues get oriented to the organization? Isn't that what those folks in Human Resources do? Who has time to connect with those colleagues in other functional areas such as marketing and engineering? Don't worry – opportunities in interacting will arise when business demands it.

The degree to which you interact with others is similar to the nature versus nurture philosophy that we hear or read about regarding human development. In scholarly articles published on this topic, *nature* typically refers to characteristics you have inherited. These characteristics may include hair color, vulnerability to disease, and personality preferences. *Nurture* typically refers to characteristics you have developed through interaction with your environment. These characteristics may include language, social perspectives, and opinions.

In a similar way, the degree to which you interact with colleagues may be driven by your natural interest to interact with others (nature) or the culture of your organization (nurture), as illustrated in Figure 7.1. Each of these situations alone can significantly increase or reduce the degree to which you interact with your colleagues. Imagine the impact to your visibility when you do not possess a natural interest in interacting with colleagues and your organization's culture does not support it – neither nature *nor* nurture are working in your favor. When you possess a strong interest in interacting with others and the culture of your organization supports such interaction, it's magic!

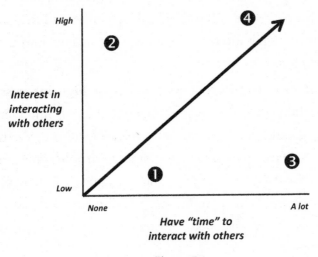

Figure 7.1

1. **No time to interact with others + low interest.** Your interaction with others is limited to meetings and conference calls. You are not interested in interacting with others and you justify that your low interaction is due to the lack of time you have at work to do anything but keep your "nose to the grindstone." You are at risk of becoming invisible in, and irrelevant to, your organization.

2. **No time to interact with others + high interest.** While you possess a sincere interest in interacting with others, the demands of your job and the culture of your organization prevent you from doing so. You are likely very frustrated by the requirements of your job, which is forcibly sequestering you in your office or workstation. Unless you find a way to satisfy your interest to interact with others, your frustration will grow into dissatisfaction, affecting your work performance in negative ways.

3. **A lot of time to interact with others + low interest.** Your job or work environment allows you many opportunities (as stated earlier, this is not unproductive time) to interact with others, yet you have little interest in doing so. You are at risk of being

viewed as an office hermit – reclusive, standoffish, and, at worst, misanthropic. Your colleagues will demonstrate little patience for your behavior and you will quickly become irrelevant to your organization.

4. **A lot of time to interact with others + high interest.** Your organization provides many opportunities to interact with colleagues and you take full advantage of these opportunities. The high degree to which you interact with colleagues is driven by your interest in doing so. You recognize the benefits (i.e., increased knowledge, influence, productivity) of interacting with colleagues and take advantage of your organization's environment to do so.

WHEN YOU CONSIDER THE FOUR AREAS HIGHLIGHTED ABOVE, WHICH OF THE FOUR AREAS DESCRIBE YOU THE BEST?

THE DIFFERENCE BETWEEN INTERACTING AND NETWORKING

There is no doubt that networking is a very important activity. As you see illustrated in Figure 7.2, and as stressed previously, networking is the primary type of interaction for individuals looking for a job or who are self-employed. By focusing on networking, these individuals build relationships that allow them to make progress in finding their next opportunity, whether that opportunity is a job or a sale.

INTERACTING VS. NETWORKING
(For individuals looking for a job or who are self-employed)

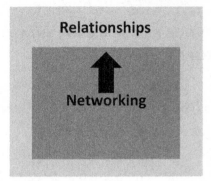

Figure 7.2

Conversely, for employed business professionals, networking becomes one of many interactions that lead to some form of relationship that raises their visibility in their workplace, as illustrated in Figure 7.3.

INTERACTING VS. NETWORKING
(Employed business professionals)

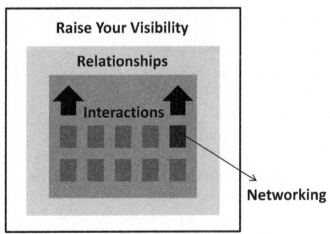

Figure 7.3

The key here is that networking is not eliminated. Employed business professionals must reallocate the time and energy they are spending (or others are telling them to spend) on networking to a much broader set of activities.

THE DIFFERENCE BETWEEN INTERACTIONS AND RELATIONSHIPS

It is important to understand the difference between an *interaction* and a *relationship* as you work to raise your visibility in your organization and industry. I defined interacting earlier in this chapter as "the degree to which you engage one-to-one with colleagues in your organization and industry." While interactions are one way to raise your visibility in your organization and industry, it is inevitable that some interactions will begin to build a relationship.

How do you define the word *relationship* as it applies to your organization? Take a moment to jot down your thoughts below.

A *RELATIONSHIP IS*_____

_____

I bet you found it difficult to quickly conjure up a definition. Relationship is one of those words that we use often, yet we find it hard to define when asked. Consider the following as a definition for "relationship:"

> A **RELATIONSHIP** IS A SERIES OF INTERACTIONS WHERE A DEPENDENCY AND/OR AN EXPECTATION IS CREATED.

You will quickly note that relationships are actually comprised of interactions. To become a relationship, however, these interactions need to create a dependency or an expectation between two or more individuals. As you work to raise your visibility in your organization and industry, some of your interactions will lead to the creation of a dependency and/or an expectation and some will not, as illustrated in Figure 7.4.

INTERACTIONS VS. RELATIONSHIPS

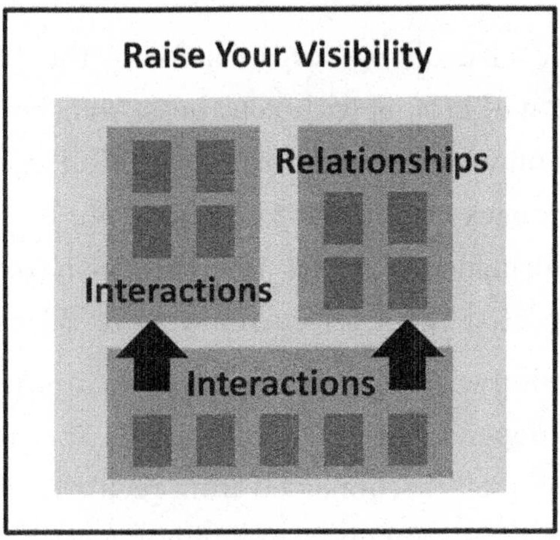

Figure 7.4

Jathan Janove is a successful attorney, author, speaker, and consultant, and each of these roles has required him to interact with colleagues in a variety of ways. Through these experiences, Jathan has built a rich perspective on the difference between interacting and building relationships. "People aren't interested in what you are selling or what you need. People are interested in building a relationship that is mutually satisfying and beneficial. The focus of the interaction shouldn't just be me or you, but us. I get to the 'us' by focusing more on the other person, asking questions, and offering ways to help them. They feel better by doing the same, and the next thing you know, a relationship is born." I've known Jathan for over ten years and my interactions with him have never felt like networking. Needless to say, Jathan excels at building relationships.

For employed business professionals, some interactions will lead to relationships, while other interactions will lead to more interactions.

Regardless of where your interactions take you, additional interactions and relationships all start with interactions; not with networking, not with relationships, but with interactions.

The Importance of Interacting with Your Boss

In today's ever-evolving organizations, the most important relationship you will have is with your boss. Your boss is accountable for the activities on which you focus. Organization leaders will come to your boss for feedback on your performance. Your boss is the author of your annual performance appraisal. Your success in your organization is dramatically impacted by the impression your boss has of you.

Your relationship with your boss is based on a series of interactions characterized by dependencies and expectations. For a variety of reasons, you often find yourself disconnected from recurring interactions with your boss, which prevents you from building a relationship. It will be difficult for your boss to have an impression of you, especially a positive one, if your interactions are limited. Your interactions with your boss may be limited due to one or more of the following reasons:

- **Time.** It is not surprising that a significant hurdle to interacting with your boss is time. In an organization where business professionals are expected to do more with less, and faster, time is at a premium. Many of your colleagues report that weeks may go by without a substantive conversation with a boss, and when a conversation does occur, it was usually due to a problem or a need for a quick piece of information. Successful business professionals find time in their busy day to connect with their boss in substantive ways and to overcome challenges in their boss's schedule by being persistent.

- **Personality.** As unique individuals, we all possess personality preferences which differentiate us. Recall the observations earlier in this chapter regarding nature or your natural interest to interact with others. Some of these personality preferences work in harmony and others create conflict. You may feel this at work when you express your feelings in ways such as "I can't get along with Bob," or "I don't know what it is, but I just don't like Karen," or "Cheryl and I seem to be from different planets." Conflicting personality preference differences between you and your boss may create a situation where you avoid spending time with your boss. For more information on the impact of personality preferences at work or to learn more about personality assessments, visit www.type-coach.com. The information and tools found at this website will help you understand personality differences in ways that help you work with colleagues effectively.

- **Geography.** In today's virtual and global workplaces, one of the biggest enemies of visibility is geographic distance. When you work in Tampa, Florida, and your boss is in Shanghai, China, or when you work from home and you are barely at the office, your ability to be visible is at significant risk. It can also be frustrating if your boss and colleagues are situated in the same building and you are the only one working at a remote location. Yet successful business professionals have found ways to stay visible with their boss, regardless of geography. These individuals realize that visibility is not just physical visibility (as in being seen), but focused more on interactions (whether physical or not). As you can see by Figure 7.5, the biggest impact is the frequency in which you interact with your boss, not geography.

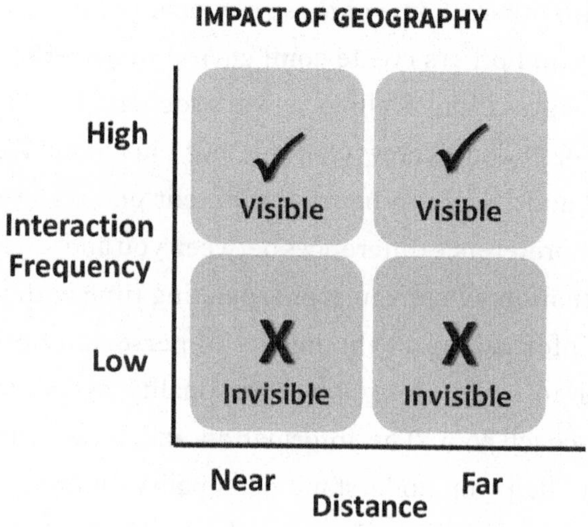

IMPACT OF GEOGRAPHY

Figure 7.5

As long as your interactions with your boss are in the high categories, you will still be visible, regardless of your geographic distance. Don't let distance become a roadblock to your relationship with your boss.

WHAT IS THE IMPACT OF FREQUENCY AND THE PACE OF CHANGE ON INTERACTING?

As we reviewed in Chapter 3, your organization is experiencing unprecedented change. The frequency of change (how *often* change occurs) and the pace of change (how *quickly* you are expected to change) are having a significant impact on you in your organization.

One significant impact is in your ability to interact and raise your visibility with colleagues. In statistics highlighted in a recent *Fast Company* article "The Four Year Career," a United States worker's median tenure in his or her current job is just 4.4 years. Concurrently, and reported in a recent *Wall Street Journal* article, the average tenure of a Fortune 500 CEO is just 4.6 years[1]. Regardless of the level in your organization, you and your colleagues are transitioning to new roles and organizations faster than ever before.

This frequency and pace of change is having a negative impact on your ability to interact and build relationships with colleagues. Networking is harder to do and less effective when colleagues and their roles change so frequently. Investing your time and energy connecting with others solely via networking translates to a lot of coffee and bagels, and before you know it, the person with whom you networked is no longer there. Any remnant of visibility that you had with this individual (along with your coffee and bagel) is gone.

A WORD ON INTERACTING VS. PARTICIPATING

The next chapter, Chapter 8, is focused on participating purposefully. You may be wondering what the difference is between interacting and participating. In the *Raise Your Visibility & Value* model, **interacting** is defined as "one-to-one" interactions with colleagues, while **participating** is defined as "one-to-many" experiences with colleagues. An example of an *interaction* is a scheduled meeting with a boss from whom you are geographically distant. An example of *participation* is asking a question at a company meeting. Interacting and participating help you raise your visibility and value to your organization in different ways.

WHAT ARE SOME WAYS YOU CAN INTERACT WITH OTHERS?

Here are some typical hurdles to interacting with others and suggestions for improving your interactions in your organization and industry.

Interaction Hurdles	Interaction Activities
I do not meet one-to-one (either in person or by phone) with my boss at least twice per month.	• Schedule a regular meeting with your boss, either in person or by phone. If you rarely speak to your boss, you are at risk of becoming irrelevant and invisible. • Schedule a regular meeting with your boss to ensure that you do not only talk when there is a problem. If you talk with your boss only when there is a problem, you are not raising your visibility with her. • Schedule time with your boss and talk about your career, progress on goals, and areas of interest which you both share.
My boss repeatedly cancels my one-to-one meetings with her.	• Ensure that you tell your boss about the importance of this time with her. It is possible that your boss feels she is helping you by giving you cancelled time back in your calendar. • Send your boss an agenda in advance, and include one to two items that require a decision from your boss. • Be persistent. If your boss cancels a meeting, immediately reschedule the meeting.
I do not meet with leaders at least two levels above me so we can get to know each other better.	• Reach out to a new leader who is one to two levels above you and new to the organization to schedule time with him, so you can get to know each other better. • Ask a colleague to join you if you are uncomfortable meeting with a leader at least two levels above you. • Take some time to think about how you and your team will work with this individual, how you and your team can help this individual, and what you and your team need from this individual. Once you have this bias, you will see the benefits of meeting in a clearer and more logical way.

Interaction Hurdles	Interaction Activities
Whatever network I have at work is comprised mostly of colleagues from my functional area (i.e. I am in Marketing and everyone in my network is from Marketing).	• Create a list of colleagues (outside of your functional area) with whom you should raise your visibility if your network is comprised solely of colleagues from your functional area. • Ask a colleague if her network expands beyond her functional area and how she went about building such a network. • Speak with your manager about volunteering for a project or committee outside of your functional area. This is a great way to meet colleagues, outside of your functional area, with whom you will share a common goal.
When a new colleague joins my immediate team, I do not schedule time with him so we can get to know each other.	• Schedule time with a new colleague (give him about a week to settle in) to ask how you can help him in his transition to his new role. • Find time to meet and welcome a new colleague (maybe over lunch!); discuss what you do, how you do it, and what you will need from him in order to do your job well. • Be persistent if your attempts to schedule time with a new employee do not materialize. Schedules can fill easily and time can pass quickly.
I telecommute almost daily or travel away from our organization's offices three or more days per week.	• Schedule time to work from your organization's offices, attend meetings in person, and meet with key colleagues. If you are never at your organization's offices, face time with your organization's leaders, your boss, and your colleagues is even more critical. • Attend all-employee meetings and your organization's social events.
I do not send a thank you email or note to colleagues.	• Buy a box of professional stationery and send out a thank-you note as soon as possible. State what your colleague did for which you are thanking him and why his actions made a difference. Close with a note of appreciation. • Create three or four thank you templates and save the templates in your draft folder. This is an easy way to quickly send a basic thank you note.

MY *INTERACT WITH OTHERS* ACTIVITY GRID

What are my activities?	How frequently will I perform this activity?	When will I start?	What is my first step?	What risk exists in making progress?	How will I address this risk?

Chapter Seven Recap

- **Interacting** is the degree to which you engage one-to-one with colleagues in your organization and industry.
- You are at risk of being a body in a chair or a voice on the phone if you are not interacting with colleagues.
- Interacting with colleagues is not about trying to find or use free-time, downtime or unproductive time. Interacting with colleagues is about engaging in activities that are already part of your workday or your organization's culture.
- By interacting with your colleagues, you:
  - Increase your knowledge of what is occurring at your fast-paced organization.
  - Build clearer opinions as to the competencies and capabilities of your colleagues.
  - Increase your productivity.
  - Influence decisions.
- The degree to which you interact with others may be impacted by your natural interest to interact with others (nature) or the culture of your organization (nurture).
- Networking is better suited for individuals who are looking for a job or are self-employed business owners.
- For employed business professionals, networking should be an activity among many, instead of being the primary activity in which they participate.
- A **relationship** is a series of interactions in which a dependency or an expectation is created.

- **Your boss** is the most important person with whom to interact. Your ability to interact with your boss may be adversely impacted by time, personality, and geography.

- Geographic distance between you and your boss is only a problem if your interaction with your boss is low. Geographically distant individuals who enjoy a high degree of interaction with their boss minimize geography as a roadblock to professional success.

- The **frequency and pace of change** in today's organizations is making it more difficult to network and build relationships. Employed business professionals must be more focused on interacting as the way to build relationships.

Chapter Eight

Visibility Accelerator #5
Participate with a Purpose

"Oh, no," Carl says to himself as an email from his boss slowly unfolds before his eyes. "Not another team building offsite!" Like a hungry ant craving a watermelon for lunch, Carl wonders how to digest this news. *Blink. Blink. Blink.* He stares at the light on his office phone, silently reminding himself that he has messages waiting. *Buzz. Buzz. Buzz.* His smartphone gently vibrates on his desk, indicating another incoming call. *Knock! Knock! Knock!* A colleague, anxious for an answer to a question she has been seeking for days, impatiently makes her presence known at Carl's closed office door. As the *blink, buzz, and knock* ricochet throughout his head, Carl feels as if he is going to burst. "This is my busiest quarter!" he silently decries. "I can't afford to be out of the office!"

Business professionals across the globe are subjected to a daily barrage of urgent email, last minute requests, and unexpected phone calls. The phrase "Your poor planning is not my emergency" silently permeates relationships between otherwise well-meaning colleagues. Business professionals are so under-resourced and overwhelmed, they are likely suffering from PTSD. Not Post-Traumatic Stress Disorder, but *professional traumatic stress disorder*[*], a condition affecting their ability to cope in complex organizations.

---

[*]A reminder that I am not a doctor, nor is this a real disorder (at least I don't think so...)

WHAT IS THE IMPACT OF MINDSET ON PARTICIPATING?

The most dramatic symptom of our newly christened PTSD is the belief that "I can't afford to be out of the office!" If you believe that this statement is true, "I can't afford to be out of the office!" is at risk of becoming a mindset that hinders your ability to raise your visibility.

You may hate Bruce Willis and scowl anytime you see one of his movies advertised. You might love eating out for lunch and organize your schedule to ensure that you make this happen. You might hate conflict and do everything you can to avoid a confrontation. Whatever your mindset might be, it is at risk of pre-determining how you interpret and respond to a situation.

> **MINDSET** IS A HABITUAL MENTAL ATTITUDE THAT DETERMINES HOW YOU WILL INTERPRET AND RESPOND TO A SITUATION.

Once "I can't afford to be out of the office!" becomes your mindset, it also becomes your way of interpreting and responding to opportunities to participate in your organization and industry. You start to believe you cannot get out of your office or workstation. You start to accept that you do not need to participate in activities at your organization in order to be successful. You stop looking for opportunities to participate. Your visibility evaporates.

It is not surprising that Carl has anchored himself to his desk chair with an invisible mindset chain. Carl believes he cannot afford to be out of his office, rationalizing that the work he has to do is preventing him from participating in activities at his organization. If you are like Carl, the "which comes first, the chicken or the egg?" metaphor is at work. Do you have the mindset that you are too busy to participate? Or, are you disinterested in participating and you are rationalizing that you cannot participate as you are too busy? Regardless of your answer, in today's fast-paced and fast-changing organizations, you must have a mindset that supports participating in organization and industry activities.

Greg Nicastro, the Executive Vice President of Development at Veracode, a leading cloud-based provider of application security, speaks passionately about the mindset of participating with a purpose. "You have so much traffic coming your way that you must be pragmatic about how you spend your time at work. You must actively shape your environment or you are at risk of your environment shaping you. A key way to be pragmatic with your time and positively shape your environment is to purposely participate in activities that help your clients and your business become very successful."

> **PARTICIPATION** IS THE DEGREE TO WHICH YOU ENGAGE IN ONE-TO-MANY ACTIVITIES WITH COLLEAGUES IN YOUR ORGANIZATION AND INDUSTRY.

WHAT IS THE DIFFERENCE BETWEEN INTERACTING AND PARTICIPATING?

Interact with Others is comprised of ways in which you can raise your visibility "one-to-one" with others. Unlike interaction, *Participate with a Purpose* is focused on "one-to-many" experiences with colleagues, as shown in Figure 8.1. Participating is comprised of activities where you raise your visibility when *many* of your colleagues are present.

INTERACTING VS. PARTICIPATING

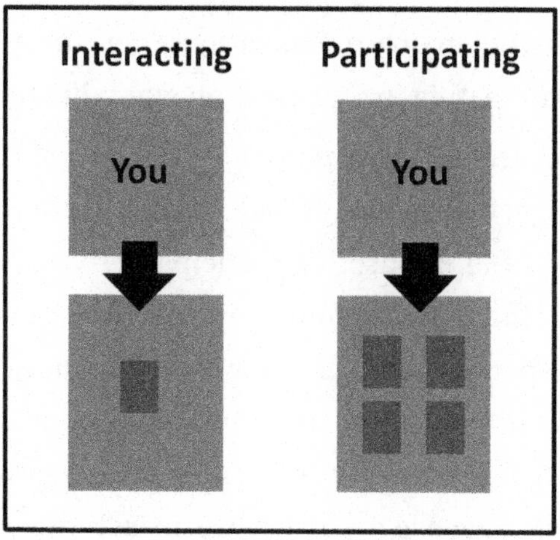

Figure 8.1

Do you find the time to participate in activities where many of your colleagues are present? Are you known for never being around? - "Has anyone seen Carl?" Are you known for never being able to attend an activity sponsored by your organization or an industry affiliation group, for one reason or another? - "I wonder why Carl never makes it to these events?" Do any of the following characteristics seem familiar to you when you think about participating with a purpose?

- You "no-show" for training classes, cancelling at the last minute because "something important" has come up.

- You claim that you can't go to all-employee meetings because it is your busiest time of the _____ (week, month, quarter, year, decade, millennium).

- You always seem to have "important" meetings or conference calls scheduled during a company activity.

- You never attend an after-hours work activity, as you always have to get home.

What is preventing you from participating in activities sponsored by your organization or industry affiliation group? Is your lack of participation a reflection of your mindset? Is it a mindset of just being too busy?

ARE YOU TOO BUSY?

As I identified in previous chapters, you are being asked to do more, faster, and with too few resources. You feel as though you are doing the jobs of three people. Your Outlook calendar is triple-booked. Recurring acquisitions add new responsibilities with no additional resources. Consolidations and downsizing shift the jobs, previously handled by your colleagues, to you. You wish a magic wand existed to take away all of the urgent email, last minute requests, and unexpected phone calls that are created by your colleagues.

You could establish agreements with colleagues on how to interact with one another in productive ways. This is a best practice used in project management when teams are about to embark on a new project. However, in day-to-day relationships that exist in fast-paced organizations, your role and responsibilities change often and agreements disappear faster than a rabbit in a hat.

Without a magic wand, it is difficult to control the behaviors of others. I am reminded of the Serenity Prayer: "God, grant me the serenity to accept the things that I cannot change, the courage to change the things that I can, and the wisdom to know the difference." You can spend all your time and expend all of your energy attempting to change the behaviors of others, without any likelihood of success. Plus, there are a lot more of them than you. Just as you think you may have made progress on modifying the disruptive behavior of a colleague, your colleague gets promoted! The best place to start is you - you and the stories you tell yourself about why you cannot participate.

WHAT IS THE IMPACT OF STORIES ON PARTICIPATING?

You may not realize it, yet you tell yourself hundreds of stories per day. I don't mean bedtime stories with princes, princesses, dragons, and castles. I don't mean stories that you share with others about what happened to you when you were a toddler, in college, or at the mall last week. I am referring to the dozens of stories that you tell yourself every day to explain why something bad happened or why another person is behaving poorly. These are the stories that solidify your mindset in ways that do not help you raise your visibility in your organization and industry.

Unfortunately, in your organization, situations frequently occur that impact you in a negative way and colleagues often do not do what you expect them to do. To rationalize why these situations or behaviors occur, you create and tell yourself stories to help you explain the inexplicable. You may be telling yourself a story about a less-than-positive interaction you just had with your boss. You are likely getting all "storied-up" to explain why a colleague you just passed in the hallway ignored your greeting of "Hi!" You might remember a recent lunch where a colleague explained her version as to why a significant change in organizational structure was abruptly announced. "Well, if you ask me..." Sound familiar? Where do these stories which you and your colleagues tell yourselves (and sometimes others) come from?

Generally speaking, your stories come from two places – your ego and your inner critic – as illustrated in Figure 8.2.

STORY SOURCES

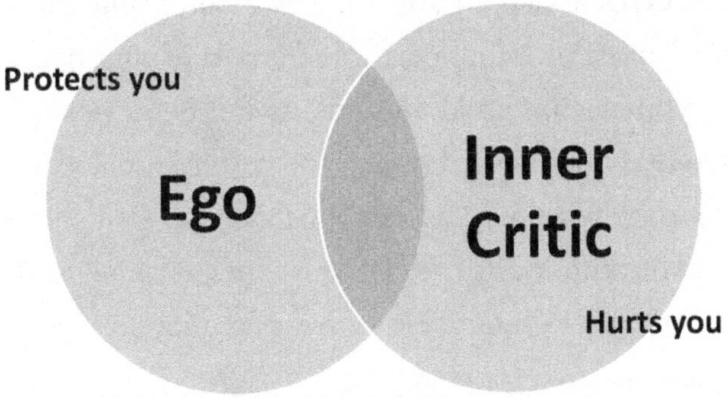

Figure 8.2

YOUR EGO

Your **ego** exists primarily in the *external* world and acts like a shield to protect your need for status, self-worth, and contribution. If something happens in the external world that attacks these needs, you create an explanation for the attack, typically due to something other than yourself. The rallying cry of your ego is "It's not me, it's them!" Here are some workplace examples of ego-based stories that may seem familiar:

- You hear that a colleague, Pat, for whom you have little respect, gets promoted to a new role.

  - **Your story -** "I can't believe they promoted Pat. Everyone knows he only got the job because he is such a brown-noser. "

- An all-employee meeting has been scheduled.

  - **Your story -** "I don't have time for this. They are not going to talk about anything important anyway."

- You do not submit an article for your organization's e-newsletter.

  - **Your story -** "What's the point? No one reads this stuff."

YOUR INNER CRITIC

Your **inner critic** exists in your *internal* world and works to erode your self-confidence. Your inner critic is the part of your personality that tells you that you are not good enough, do not deserve something you received, or could have handled a situation better. It thrives on questions like "What's wrong with me?" or conclusions like "What an idiot!" The rallying cry of your inner critic is "It's not them, it's me!" Here are some workplace examples of inner critic stories that may sound familiar:

- A hiring manager never calls you back after an interview.
  - **Your story -** "I bet they found a better candidate. I must have interviewed horribly!"
- You send an email to a colleague to follow-up on two previous outreaches that went unanswered.
  - **Your story -** "Did something I write offend him?"
- You do not join an industry association group.
  - **Your story -** "I hate going to these meetings. I never know anyone."

Do these ego and inner critic stories sound familiar? Do you see yourself thinking these stories or stories like them? Do you have a sense of how frequently your ego raises a shield to protect you or how often your inner critic corrodes your self-confidence?

My goal is not to go "all psychological on you" and start throwing around fancy and important sounding concepts like *ego* and *inner critic*. If this were my intent, this book would cost a lot more. My goal is to introduce the concepts of ego and inner critic so that you can build your self-awareness of when they rise up and assault your thought processes.

UNDERSTANDING YOUR EGO AND YOUR INNER CRITIC

IMAGINE THAT YOU ARE ON TRIAL BECAUSE YOU DID NOT TO ATTEND AN ALL-EMPLOYEE MEETING. IN OUR MOCK TRIAL, YOUR **EGO IS YOUR DEFENSE ATTORNEY** AND YOUR **INNER CRITIC IS THE PROSECUTING ATTORNEY**.

YOUR **DEFENSE ATTORNEY (EGO)** STANDS BEFORE THE JURY OF YOUR PEERS AND MAKES AN IMPASSIONED PLEA FOR YOUR INNOCENCE. "LADIES AND GENTLEMEN OF THE JURY, IT IS NOT MY CLIENT'S FAULT THAT HE WAS UNABLE TO ATTEND THE ALL-EMPLOYEE MEETING. THE ANNOUNCEMENT FOR THE MEETING WAS SENT OUT TOO LATE FOR MY CLIENT TO CHANGE HIS SCHEDULE. ON TOP OF THAT, THE LAST THREE ALL-EMPLOYEE MEETINGS THAT MY CLIENT HAS ATTENDED HAVE BEEN DUDS. WITH BORING SPEAKERS AND ENDLESS POWERPOINT PRESENTATIONS, THESE MEETINGS ARE A REAL WASTE OF MY CLIENT'S PRECIOUS TIME. HE'S FAR TOO BUSY! MY CLIENT WAS FULLY JUSTIFIED IN NOT ATTENDING THIS MEETING AND I DEMAND YOU FIND HIM INNOCENT!"

NEXT, THE **PROSECUTING ATTORNEY (INNER CRITIC)**, RISES FROM HIS CHAIR AND MAKES HIS IMPASSIONED PLEA FOR THE JURY TO FIND YOU GUILTY. "ESTEEMED MEMBERS OF THE JURY. WHAT A GREAT STORY THE DEFENDANT IS TELLING HIMSELF. THE DEFENDANT IS ONE OF THE MOST DISORGANIZED INDIVIDUALS THIS OFFICER OF THE COURT HAS EVER SEEN. HE FORGOT TO SCHEDULE THE ALL-EMPLOYEE MEETING IN HIS CALENDAR. HIS ORGANIZATION SKILLS ARE SO BAD, HE DOES NOT DESERVE TO BE IN THIS COURTROOM TODAY. ON TOP OF THAT, HE HATES SOCIALIZING WITH HIS COLLEAGUES – HE NEVER KNOWS WHAT TO SAY AND IS ALWAYS AFRAID HE IS GOING TO SAY SOMETHING STUPID. WHAT A LOSER! I DEMAND YOU FIND THE DEFENDANT GUILTY!"

WHAT IS THE OUTCOME OF THIS TRIAL? WELL, YOU GET TO BE THE **JUDGE** TOO!

How can you easily identify a story that you are telling yourself? You know you are about to create a story if you find yourself starting a sentence with one of the following:

- "I think..."
- "My guess would be..."

- "Sounds to me like ..."
- "It seems to me that..."
- "Well, if you ask me..."

For example, a colleague asks you for your thoughts about Pat being promoted to a new role. Your story may sound like one of the following:

- *"I think...* they picked Pat because he sits right down the hallway from Susan (the hiring manager) and Pat sees her every day. We're disadvantaged because we are all located in different parts of the country."
- *"My guess would be...* that Pat was threatening to leave and the company didn't want to have to deal with that."
- *"Sounds to me like...* Pat's been brown-nosing the right people."
- *"It seems to me that...* this company likes picking men for key positions."
- *"Well, if you ask me...* Pat must have done someone somewhere a big favor."

It is important to note that stories are not lies. We sometimes hear colleagues say, "He's just lying to himself." A lie is typically an untrue statement created with the intent to deceive or create a false or misleading impression. Since you believe your stories to be true and have not been created to deceive, stories are not lies.

Take a few minutes to identify stories that you may have told yourself recently. In the boxes below, identify at least three situations which occurred within the last day or so that had a negative impact on you. I've created a personal example as a reference. What was the story that you told yourself as to why a person (friend, family member, or colleague) behaved the way that he did or why a situation occurred as it did? You can use the space provided in the following boxes or use your own piece of paper.

What behavior or situation recently occurred that had a negative impact on you?	What is the story that you told yourself to explain why this behavior or situation occurred?	Is the story that you told yourself coming from your ego or your inner critic?
The postman doesn't put the mail all the way into our free-standing mailbox.	He is in a rush or he is being sloppy.	Ego!
The postman doesn't put the mail all the way into our free-standing mailbox.	It must be too hard to put mail in the mailbox – I've got to fix that.	Inner critic!

Were you able to identify at least three? If not, pay attention to experiences you have over the next day and identify situations, behaviors, and stories as you go. Did you have more than three? If so, you are representative of the majority of the population who tell themselves dozens of stories per day.

At best, the stories that you tell yourself may help you temporarily navigate a challenging situation or maintain your self-esteem. At worst, these stories lead you to incorrect conclusions and have a negative domino effect on subsequent decisions. As you will read in the next section, the stories that you tell yourself impact your behavior – behavior that is not helping you raise your visibility in your organization and industry.

What is the Impact of Limiting Beliefs on Participating?

Ego and inner critic stories create what leadership coaches commonly call "limiting beliefs."

> A **LIMITING BELIEF** IS A STORY THAT YOU TELL YOURSELF,
> WHETHER TRUE OR FALSE, THAT DOES NOT HELP YOU.

Regardless of whether the stories that you tell yourself are coming from your ego or your inner critic, your limiting beliefs have the following characteristics in common:

- You tell limiting beliefs primarily to yourself, although you may share your beliefs with others at a later time.

- You create limiting beliefs to fill in missing information.

- You believe your limiting beliefs are true, whether they are true or false.

- You make behavioral choices based on your limiting beliefs.

Since your limiting beliefs inform your behavioral choices, as illustrated in Figure 8.3, consider the impact that the stories you are telling yourself have on your behavior.

THE IMPACT OF LIMITING BELIEFS

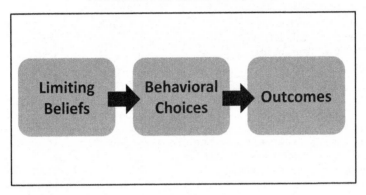

Figure 8.3

Essentially, you will make behavioral choices based on information that you believe to be true. Whether your behavior is conscious (purposefully chosen) or unconscious (the natural way you react to something), some type of behavior will surface.

Think about the **ego** story examples previously provided, and consider how a limiting belief played a role. In its effort to shield you from external behavior that is negatively impacting you, your ego fills in information that may or may not be true, and where limited information exists. Remember the rallying cry of your ego – "It's not me, it's them!" Let's look at the ego-based story examples from earlier and apply the limiting belief model to them.

What is the behavior or situation?	What is the story you tell yourself?	Is the story true or false?	How do you behave?	Does this behavior help or hurt you?
You hear that a colleague for whom you have little respect gets promoted to a new role.	"I can't believe they promoted Pat. Everyone knows he only got the job because he is such a brown-noser."	You don't know why Pat was selected.	You start acting negatively or dismissively towards Pat.	👎
An all-employee meeting has been scheduled.	"I don't have time for this. They are not going to talk about anything important anyway."	You don't know everything that will be discussed.	You do not go to the meeting.	👎
You do not submit an article for your organization's e-newsletter.	"What's the point? No one reads this stuff."	You don't know to what extent anyone reads the e-newsletter.	You do not submit an article.	👎

Concurrently, a limiting belief may take the form of your **inner critic** filling in information where limited information exists. Let's look at the inner critic-based examples from earlier and apply the limiting belief model to them.

What is the behavior or situation?	What is the story you tell yourself?	Is the story true or false?	How do you behave?	Does this behavior help or hurt you?
A hiring manager never calls you back after an interview that you thought went well.	"I bet they found a better candidate. I must have interviewed horribly!"	You don't know the recruiter's reason for not getting back to you. You don't know his opinion on how you interviewed.	You become "gun-shy" and stop interviewing.	👎
You send an email to a colleague to follow-up on two previous outreaches to which your colleague has never responded.	"Did something I write offend him?"	You don't know why your colleague has not responded to your outreaches.	You stop trying to contact your colleague and never obtain the information you need.	👎
You do not join an industry association group.	"I hate going to these meetings. I never know anyone."	You don't know if you will know anyone or not.	You do not join the industry association group.	👎

You adopt a limiting belief that a meeting is not valuable, so you don't attend. You don't think anyone reads your organization's newsletter, so you don't submit an article. You don't believe you will know anyone at a meeting, so you don't join the industry affiliation group. By filling-in missing information with limiting beliefs, you are limiting your options in ways that do not help you. Not only are you lessening your options, you are allowing limiting beliefs to creep into your mind. You begin to feel:

- Negative

- Disenfranchised

- De-Energized

Take a few minutes to identify limiting beliefs that you may have told yourself recently. In the boxes below, repeat the three stories that you identified in the earlier section that is focused on stories. Take a few moments to know whether the story you told yourself is true or false and your subsequent behaviors. You can use the space provided in the following boxes or use your own piece of paper.

What is the behavior or situation?	What is the story you told yourself?	Was the story true or false?	How did you behave?	Did the behavior help or hurt you?

If the story you are telling yourself about participating is not true, you are at risk of behaving in a way that does not help you raise your visibility in your organization and industry. What can a business professional do about this? How do you combat this onslaught of stories that you create for yourself that are not helping you?

USE THE BEST OPTION MODEL TO COMBAT LIMITING BELIEFS

Nail-biting is widely known as a behavior in which many participate unconsciously. This is especially challenging if you are attempting to stop biting your nails. While you aspire to stop this habit, you often find yourself biting your nails without consciously choosing to do so. Perhaps you are watching a movie or reading a book when you suddenly catch yourself biting your nails. Suddenly, you whip your hand away from your mouth while silently cursing yourself. The first step is not to stop biting your nails - the first step is to recognize when it is about to happen. This way, you can consciously choose what to do next.

Similarly, if you want to make progress combating limiting beliefs, you first have to build your skill in consciously recognizing when a limiting belief is occurring. The goal of this chapter is to help you build that skill set. You have made significant progress if you have increased your ability to recognize when you are creating a limiting belief that reduces your likelihood of participating in an activity created by your organization or industry.

To combat a limiting belief, you need to follow the five steps illustrated in Figure 8.4:

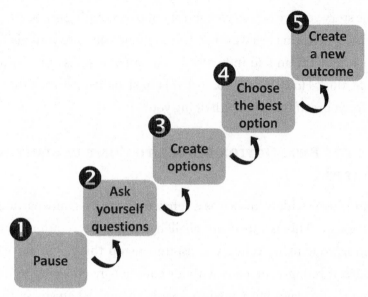

Figure 8.4

1. **Pause.** Demonstrate your skill to consciously recognize that a limiting belief is being created.

2. **Ask yourself questions.** Use the following questions to assess your limiting belief:

   - How true is the limiting belief I am telling myself?

   - Is my limiting belief being generated by my ego or by my inner critic?

   - If I weren't pausing and asking myself questions, in what behavior would I participate?

   - Does this behavior help me?

3. **Create options.** Think about and identify additional options on how to behave.

4. **Choose the best option.** Of the options I have identified, which option (including my limiting belief option) is in my best interest?

5. **Create a new outcome.** Take action based on the best option you have selected.

Using the Best Option Model to Combat a Limiting Belief

Carl is going to use the best option model to combat a limiting belief regarding his attendance at an upcoming all-employee meeting. Carl chooses not to attend because he told himself the following story –

"I don't have time for this. They are not going to talk about anything important anyway."

1. **Pause.** Carl has built his skill at recognizing when he is telling himself a story and is generating a limiting belief. He takes a few moments to pause and reflect.

2. **Ask yourself questions.** By asking himself some questions, Carl comes to the following conclusions:

   - The limiting belief I was telling myself is not true. I can make time if I have to and it is possible that the topics will be important.

   - The limiting belief is being generated by my ego, telling me the meeting would be a waste of my precious time. ("My time is too important to waste attending a meeting!")

   - If I hadn't paused to ask myself questions, I would not be going to the meeting.

   - Not attending an all-employee meeting does not help me.

3. **Create options.** Carl thinks about this situation for a little while and he identifies the following options:

   - Not attend (my current behavior if I accept my limiting belief)

   - Revisit my schedule to identify if I can move any appointments

   - Request an extension of a deliverable on which I was planning to work

4. **Choose the best option.** Carl considers his options and chooses to ask for an extension for a deliverable on which he was planning to work during the all-employee meeting.

5. **Create a new outcome.** Carl obtains approval for an extension and attends the all-employee meeting.

The goal of the **best option model** is not to figure out what options might exist for an individual in order to create a new outcome. Options are dependent on the nature of the situation, and these situations and options are endless. The goal of this exercise is to build a skill around using the **best option model**. As you can see illustrated in Figure 8.5, different options lead us to different outcomes and all of our choices come with some degree of risk.

In the **best option model,** your goal is to close the **risk gap**. The risk gap is the space between the outcomes created by the choices you make. A path selected based upon a limited belief creates great risk for you. A path selected based upon a purposeful choice reduces the risk for you. Reduce your risk gap by choosing the best option.

DIFFERENT STORIES, DIFFERENT PATHS

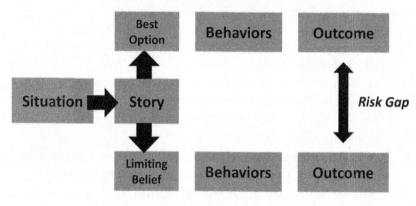

Figure 8.5

IN WHAT WAYS CAN I PARTICIPATE?

The title of this chapter is *Participate with a Purpose* and the ways in which you can participate one-to-many are endless. In the *Raise Your Visibility & Value* model, it is assumed that there are an infinite number of ways to participate with a purpose. Of them, networking is just one. Recall that networking is the number one activity on which individuals looking for a job and individuals focused on business development should focus. However, networking is just one of many activities for employed business professionals. This is where you and your employed colleagues get stuck. You over-invest in networking because this is where all of your colleagues and all of the articles tell you to focus. Yet, as an employed business professional, there are so many other activities that exist which can help you achieve your goals faster and more effectively.

When you think about participating with a purpose, consider organizing your activities into the following categories:

- Contribute
- Engage
- Attend
- Lead

CONTRIBUTE

When you contribute, you are identifying activities in which you provide information or content to others in your organization and industry. Examples of places to contribute include:

- Podcasts
- Blogs
- Newsletters/e-newsletters
- Websites
- White papers

ENGAGE

When you engage, you are identifying activities in which you participate and interact with others in your organization and industry *with a requirement that you provide specific content or deliverables.* Examples of ways to engage include:

- Team membership in a project within your functional area.

- Team membership in a project outside of your functional area.
- Membership in a organization committee (i.e., philanthropic, employee activity).

ATTEND

When you attend, you are identifying activities in which you participate and interact with others in your organization and industry, *without a requirement that you provide specific content or deliverables.* Examples of activities to attend include:

- Team meetings
- Team building events
- All-employee meetings
- Training programs

LEAD

When you lead, you are identifying activities in which you participate and interact with others in your organization and industry from a leadership perspective. Not only are you providing specific content and deliverables, you are ensuring that others achieve their commitments as well. Examples of ways to lead others include:

- Conducting a training class on either soft skills (i.e., conflict management) or technical skills (i.e., your organization's uniquely configured customer relationship management software).
- Leading a project within your functional area.
- Leading a project outside of your functional area.
- Chairing a committee.

Whether you contribute, engage, attend or lead, participating with a purpose is a critical way to raise your visibility in your organization and your industry.

WHAT ARE SOME WAYS YOU CAN PARTICIPATE WITH A PURPOSE?

Here are some typical hurdles to participating with a purpose and suggestions for improving your participation in your organization and industry.

Participation Hurdles	Participation Activities
I do not ask questions when attending podcasts hosted by my organization.	• Ask whoever is hosting the podcast, in advance of the podcast, if there are any questions which he knows need to be asked. Asking a relevant question is a great way to comfortably get involved. • Kick around a few possible questions with some colleagues before the next podcast. • Schedule the podcast on your calendar. You can't ask questions if you are not in attendance. Check your organization's website for upcoming podcast days and times.
I do not seek "stretch" assignments outside of my immediate team.	• Seek out a "stretch" assignment outside of your immediate team. • Speak with a colleague who is or has participated in a "stretch" assignment and ask for her advice on how to pursue such an assignment. • Contact a colleague in your organization's Leadership Development department for already existing programs that help colleagues obtain a "stretch" assignment. • Schedule some time with your manager to discuss the possibility for a "stretch" assignment.
I am not a team leader on a project outside of my immediate team.	• Talk with your manager about a leadership role in a current or upcoming project outside of your immediate team. • Speak with a colleague who is currently the team leader outside of her immediate team. Ask her about the experience and how she went about being selected to lead a project outside of her immediate team. • Create an incentive for yourself to lead a team outside of your immediate team and add this activity to your annual performance goals or professional development plan.

Participation Hurdles	Participation Activities
I do not help train others within our organization on technical skills topics (i.e., technical systems, organization processes, software).	• Contact your training organization to see if there are opportunities to train others in your organization on technical skill topics. • Speak with a colleague to gauge interest in co-training others within your organization on technical skills topics. Don't go it alone! • Ask your training organization to allow you to do a portion of an existing program training others in your organization on technical skills topics. This is a great way to "put your toe in the water."
I am not a team member on a project within my immediate team.	• Talk with your manager about a role in a current or upcoming team project. Working on a team with your colleagues can provide you great visibility. • Speak with a colleague on your team who is currently on a team project. Ask him about the experience and how he went about getting on the project team. • Ask if you can help a team in a small way that will not monopolize your time. Starting small is a great way to participate with a purpose.
I do not contribute information to my company newsletter, e-newsletter, or website.	• Create a goal to contact whoever publishes/manages your organization's newsletter/e-newsletter and ask how contributions are solicited and accepted. • Suggest a recurring contribution to your organization's newsletter/e-newsletter focused on information from your functional area (i.e., finance, marketing, human resources) that can be helpful to others. • Brainstorm with one or more colleagues on topics you can write for your organization's newsletter/e-newsletter.
I do not participate on a committee that supports my organization. (i.e., employee activity, scholarship, corporate giving).	• Speak with your manager about your participation on a committee that is valuable to the organization. • Contact a colleague who is a member of a committee and learn about his/her experiences and recommendations. • Investigate committee membership now, yet join later. This way, you can be better prepared to handle additional responsibilities and time commitments. • Speak with your manager about starting a committee that does not currently exist in your organization. Perhaps you have not joined a committee at work because the topics do not interest you.

MY *PARTICIPATE WITH A* PURPOSE ACTIVITY GRID

What are my activities?	How frequently will I perform this activity?	When will I start?	What is my first step?	What risk exists in making progress?	How will I address this risk?

Chapter Eight Recap

- **Participation** is the degree to which you engage in one-to-many activities with colleagues in your organization and industry.

- **Mindset** is a habitual mental attitude that determines how you will interpret and respond to a situation.

- Once "I can't afford to be out of the office!" becomes your mindset, you start to believe you cannot get out of your office or workstation and participate with others.

- Your days are very busy and it is difficult to control the behaviors of others. The best place to start is with you and the **stories** you tell yourself about why you cannot participate.

- You tell yourself dozens of stories every day to explain why something bad happened or why another person is behaving poorly.

- The stories that you tell yourself come from two places – your ego and your inner critic.

  - Your **ego** exists in the external world and protects your need for status, self-worth, and contribution. Your ego's rallying cry is "It's not me, it's them!"

  - Your **inner critic** exists in the internal world and works to erode your self-confidence. Your inner critic's rallying cry is "It's not them, it's me!"

- Ego and inner critic stories create limiting beliefs. A **limiting belief** is a story that you tell yourself, whether true or false, that does not help you.

- You make choices regarding participation, based on your limiting beliefs, that are not helping you.

- To combat limiting beliefs, follow the **best option model** comprised of the following steps:
  - Pause
  - Ask yourself questions
  - Create options
  - Choose the best option
  - Create a new outcome
- The goal of the best option model is to close the risk gap. The **risk gap** is the space between the least and most optimal choice for participation.
- When you participate, you will generally do so in one of the following ways:
  - Contribute
  - Engage
  - Attend
  - Lead

CHAPTER NINE

Visibility Accelerator #6
Engage with Industry Associations

Unbeknownst to his colleagues, Carl is an avid diarist. Maybe it is his legal training, which advocates the importance of note-taking. Maybe Carl logs his daily activities as a therapeutic way to make his frenzied and ever-changing organization less blurry. If it were possible to do a word search of Carl's diary for the word "meeting," you would find the following recent entries:

March 12, 2017

"Dear Diary – I am looking forward to my first meeting tonight as a new member of the Software Development Association. I can't wait to meet some colleagues who do what I do."

March 13, 2017

'Dear Diary – I can't believe that I did not make it to the meeting last night. Just as I was getting ready to leave the office, my boss stopped by and asked if I could spend a few minutes speaking with one of our key customers. What I thought would be a ten-minute conference call became a ninety-minute conference call. Oh, well, I'll make next month's meeting."

April 17, 2017

"Dear Diary – I am really excited about attending my first meeting of the Software Development Association. I missed last month's meeting and as long as I don't answer my phone as I am leaving, I know I will make it!"

April 18, 2017

"Dear Diary – Just as I was getting ready to leave the office, I answered my phone. My boss wanted to know the status of the Smith complaint. What I thought would be a ten-minute update turned into a ninety-minute discussion. Not only did the discussion result in a ton of revisions to the work I had already submitted, I ended up missing my meeting again. I will definitely make next month's meeting."

May 15, 2017

"Dear Diary – I am going to make tonight's meeting if it kills me. My colleagues keep telling me how good the speakers are, and how much they are learning. I'm really looking forward to it."

May 16, 2017

"Dear Diary – I was so busy at work yesterday that by the time I picked my head up from my desk, it was already 8:00 pm. Not only was I too late to get to the meeting, I was too tired to go anyway. Trying to attend these meetings is becoming more wishful thinking than a reality. I think I'll just forget about them and focus on my work. Who has the time anyway?"

Like Carl, your desire to attend an industry association meeting probably feels like a dream. Your ability to attend industry meetings during your workday, after your workday ends, or on the weekend is compromised in the following ways:

- **Lack of energy.** You are so exhausted by the demands of your job that the thought of getting excited and energized for an industry activity, especially after your workday ends, is beyond your capacity. By the time the clock strikes 6:00 pm, you are physically tired and mentally tapped-out.
- **Lack of time.** You have too much to do! So many of your colleagues are depending on you to do your job that the idea of taking time

away from work seems impossible. How can you find time when your calendar is double- or triple-booked? Your fear of the volume of work waiting for you when you return from being away from the office is a major disincentive to attending a meeting.

- **Lack of information.** You are so deep into the activities, tasks, and requirements of your job that you are not even aware of industry activities that are going on around you. You are more focused on joining a conference call or getting to a conference room than you are on attending an industry conference. Even if you wanted to attend an industry event, you would not know where to find an event to attend.

- **Lack of support.** If you register for an industry meeting or event, your attendance is at risk due to last minute "issues" at your organization. An urgent phone call from your boss politely asking you to alter your plans is more likely than you attending the industry event. Or, your boss believes that engaging with your industry is something you do after the workday ends or on the weekend. If you do attend an industry event, you are distracted due to an onslaught of emails and phone calls from work. While it is nice to be needed by your colleagues, you wonder why they can't seem to get along without you, even for just one day.

You are not alone. In today's fast-paced and fast-changing organizations, it is hard to find the time, energy, and support to attend industry events. However, in addition to raising your visibility *within* your organization, it is more important than ever to raise your visibility *outside* of your organization as well.

> **ENGAGING WITH INDUSTRY ASSOCIATIONS** IS THE DEGREE TO WHICH YOU INTERACT AND PARTICIPATE WITH COLLEAGUES *OUTSIDE* OF YOUR ORGANIZATION.

Your professional success rests with the degree to which you raise your visibility in your organization *and* industry. You could spend all of your time being visible within your organization at the expense of industry visibility. However, when you are only visible in your organization, you miss opportunities for professional development and opportunities to build richer relationships with industry colleagues. Or, you could spend all of your time being visible within your industry at the expense of organization visibility. However, when you are invisible in your organization, you miss opportunities for advancement, and your voice is not sought out to help shape decisions and strategies.

Maximum visibility resides in a combination of organization *and* industry visibility, as illustrated in Figure 9.1.

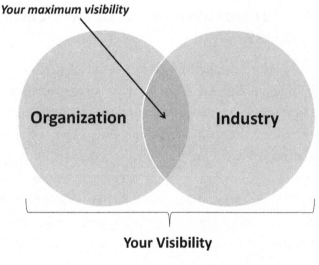

Figure 9.1

The blend of organization and industry visibility differs from person to person. Whether the time you spend raising your visibility in your organization and industry is divided "50/50%, 70/30% or 90/10%", the percentage of time you spend cultivating your organization or industry visibility is significantly less important than *cultivating both*.

If you are like most of my clients, you spend little time raising your visibility in your organization and industry, and your invisibility comes back to haunt you. One day, you arrive at work to find out that a colleague was promoted to a position you coveted. Another day, you are called to a meeting to hear that your department is being restructured, and you are now reporting to an individual for whom you have little respect. Still another day, you come back from lunch, and your boss unexpectedly stops by, closes your door, and tells you that your position has been eliminated. Many of my clients found out the hard way they were invisible in their organization and industry because they never attempted to raise their visibility until they lost their job. Therefore, if you are waiting until you need to engage with your industry versus engaging now, it is already too late.

WHAT ARE THE REASONS TO ENGAGE WITH INDUSTRY ASSOCIATIONS?

A number of reasons exist with industry associations in your effort to raise your visibility. As Chief Executive Officer of the Northeast Human Resources Association, the largest human resources association in the Northeast with over 2,000 members, Tracy Burns knows firsthand how industry association engagement can raise your visibility, positively impacting you and your career. "It is very clear to me that the key differentiator for professional success today is building relationships with colleagues you meet through industry associations," says Tracy. "I have seen dozens of highly-qualified human resources professionals who don't know what is going on in the industry, don't stay current on best practices, and, quite frankly, don't know their colleagues. I took a different route. By engaging with industry associations early in my career, I benefited in endless ways. Through my relationships with colleagues, I've been connected to job, teaching, and speaking opportunities, introduced to my master's program, and provided invaluable professional advice – on and off the record! By engaging with industry associations, I always felt that I had career options."

It is important to think about and identify *your reasons* to engage with your industry. Engaging with your industry without a compelling reason will not be sufficient to muster the energy, support, and time needed to do so. You can engage with your industry for a variety of reasons, including the following:

- **Identify talent.** Due to changing demographics, the employment marketplace continues to be highly competitive. Your organization's fast-changing technologies make some skills instantly obsolete, and some skills inordinately valuable. Your organization's fast-changing business model requires talent in new locations across the globe. Your organization's strategic growth demands that a talent pipeline exists at all times, not just when a need arises. While talent is easier to find due to technological advances (i.e., resume readers) and social media (i.e., LinkedIn), talent is harder to land as everyone else is using the same technology and social media tools. Industry associations provide rich reserves of talent that you can tap to help you and your organization fill the pipeline. Some of these individuals may be between jobs, while others are actively and happily employed. Regardless of their status, you will meet many experienced colleagues who can fill current or future needs through industry associations.

- **Hear best practices.** Industry associations provide services to their members that focus on building community, providing education, and creating opportunity through events such as:

  - **Meetings.** Industry associations host member meetings on a recurring basis. These meetings may include opportunities to raise your visibility with colleagues, discussions regarding the industry, and presentations by industry experts.

  - **Workshops and Webinars.** Industry associations host workshops and webinars for members, usually with an external speaker or facilitator, to help members build their skills and learn new information.

- **Panels.** Industry associations host panel presentations comprised of industry leaders (maybe you!) to share information and create dialogue.

- **Conferences.** Industry associations host one- to three-day conferences designed to bring together thought leaders and vendors to showcase the very best the industry has to offer. The downside is that industry conferences are usually located at beautiful destinations, held in gorgeous conference centers, and surrounded by luxurious accommodations. Not a bad downside, right?

- **Introduce best practices.** Perhaps you are attending an industry event during the workday. Perhaps your organization has paid for your industry association dues or registration fees. If you are attending industry events where information is being shared, it is expected that you introduce best practices back at your workplace that will help your organization achieve its goals. If you don't share what you are experiencing at an industry event with your boss or introduce best practices to your organization, your boss may begin to question the value of your participation. Many of your colleagues have heard about how to implement a Six Sigma process improvement, how to integrate changes to Generally Accepted Accounting Principles, and how to transition to a WordPress website at an industry meeting. Hearing about these best practices is interesting – introducing them back to your organization is priceless.

- **Meet experts.** You have a lot going on at your organization, and a key asset to accelerating your progress is meeting someone who has already done what you are doing. Whatever you are attempting to introduce or implement at your organization, there is someone who has "been there, done that." Industry associations are fantastic places to meet colleagues who can provide you valuable insights, compelling lessons, and meaningful recommendations to ensure your success. In some cases, the experience of a colleague pays for your membership many times over.

- **Demonstrate openness.** Your fast-paced organization demands your attention and effort 100% of the time, but your fast-paced industry also makes it challenging to stay current. By engaging with your industry, you demonstrate to your internal clients and colleagues that you are not satisfied with the status quo. If you want to keep your organization on the cutting edge, you have to stay sharp. Industry associations are a great place to sharpen your edge.

WILL MY BOSS THINK I AM LOOKING FOR A JOB?

When you work to raise your visibility in your industry, many of you may feel you are at risk of creating an impression with your boss that you are looking for a new job opportunity. Many industry events are advertised as networking events where you meet colleagues from within your industry. Your boss may feel that you will meet a new colleague who will lure you away to a new opportunity with promises of wealth and fame.

The best way to minimize this perception is to always be engaging with industry associations, not just when you urgently need to do so. What is the impact of engaging with an industry association proactively versus reactively? In the early stages of the banking crisis that reached its peak in 2009, an area of interest for banking regulators was a financial institution's records retention program, and specifically, the bank's strategy for shredding information. If the financial institution had a long-standing records retention program which included a shredding schedule (proactive), the bank regulators applauded them. If the financial institution did not have a records retention program and suddenly began shredding information upon the arrival of the regulators (reactive), the regulators eviscerated them.

What lesson can you apply to your participation in industry associations? If you are a recurring member of your industry, your attendance at an industry conference or your participation at an industry meeting will not raise suspicion. But, if you suddenly start to participate at industry meetings, your boss will become suspicious. By *always* participating, you do not create distracting or unfounded suspicions.

Another example of proactive versus reactive behavior exists within LinkedIn. Nothing will arouse the suspicion of your boss faster than a sudden increase in your frequency of updating your LinkedIn profile, even if you turn off the public notification functionality. Had you always had an updated profile (proactive), your updates would seem like a natural and recurring behavior. A sudden surge in updates on your LinkedIn profile due to being passed over for a promotion (reactive) will draw suspicion faster than a cat with a mouth full of feathers standing next to an empty birdcage.

HOW DO I BALANCE WORK AND INDUSTRY ASSOCIATION ENGAGEMENT?

Balancing work and industry association engagement in your busy organization is not easy. Engaging with industry associations can become harder if your boss does not support the concept. Your boss may feel that industry association meetings are just social or networking events "dressed-up" to look like a work-related event. Your boss may believe that engaging with your industry is not a productive use of time. Your boss may think that any industry-related activities should be done "off-the-clock." If your boss has any of these perspectives, his lack of support can be a significant hurdle to your efforts to engage with your industry.

In order to ensure that your boss's mindset is a hurdle rather than a roadblock, follow these steps:

- **Be open with your boss.** Your participation in an industry association should not be a secret. In order to reduce the stress that your boss or your organization may create due to your membership in an industry association, be open with your boss regarding any industry affiliations in which you are a member. Share with your boss that while you anticipate it will be infrequent, you will be interested in attending an industry meeting or conference that might occur during a workday. Confirm with your boss that you will let her know immediately so that your attendance is not a surprise to her.

- **Ask for support.** Once your boss is aware that you might attend an industry association meeting or conference during the workday, ask for his support. Ensure he understands that the meeting is work-related, and remind him of the benefits I previously listed for attending an industry event:

  - You will network with other business professionals in order to **identify talent** for key open-positions in your department.

  - You will network with **industry experts** who might have insights on how to plan and implement a big project that is scheduled to start next year.

  - You will learn and bring back to the organization **best practices** that can help the organization achieve its short- and long-term goals.

  - You will accelerate your **professional development**, increasing the value that you provide to the organization.

- **Plan for your absence.** Once you are committed to attend an industry event that occurs during the workday, ensure that you plan for your absence. Often, your boss will feel less angst if she knows that pending work is being completed while you are away. Delegate key tasks to your subordinates, and ask a peer to act as a "point-person" for your team in your absence. This ensures that the work you are responsible for gets done. By identifying a peer to act as your point-person during your absence, you also reduce the risk of drowning in a flood of email and phone calls from subordinates, clients, and bosses.

- **Deliver on your plan.** In order to ensure that you can attend future events during the workday, you must deliver on your plan. Nothing will shoot down a future request to attend an industry event during the workday faster than the memory of a debacle that occurred during your last absence. Assuming that your plan worked, ensure your boss is aware that your team rose to the occasion.

How Do I Get My Company to Pay for My Industry Association Membership?

An important mindset for you, your boss, and your organization is that your membership in an industry association is *work-related*. This is not an extracurricular activity. The benefits to you and your organization, as we reviewed in the prior section, are compelling and numerous.

Once you convince your boss that your membership and attendance is work-related, you want to have your organization pay for your membership or registration fees. Ideally, your boss has budgeted money for industry memberships and meeting registrations. If not, help your boss become proactive by allocating dollars during the budget planning cycle for professional development and industry memberships. The fastest way to stop a conversation regarding your organization paying your fees is that there is no money budgeted.

How do you start? You could write a memo similar to the example illustrated in Figure 9.2, or use the key points from this example as talking points for a conversation.

Sample Memo to Your Boss Regarding
Your Attendance at an Industry Event

Dear Sharon,

I am interested in attending a professional development workshop being hosted by the Software Development Association (SDA). The workshop is on Tuesday, April 10, starting at 8:00am and ending at 4:00pm.

The SDA is a global organization dedicated to the professional development of business professionals in the software industry. As I continue to grow my career with our organization, I believe attending this event has the following advantages:

- There will be over 100 professionals in attendance at this workshop.

- I would like to use this opportunity to search for candidates for the open Legal Assistant role.

- I would like to recap best practices that I learn during the workshop and share them with you. Together, we may identify a couple of best practices that we can implement here.

- I want to seek out a colleague who is familiar with the new invoicing platform to which we will be moving in three years. I anticipate this colleague can provide us some information and advice about his/her experiences.

During my absence, I plan to have Marc be the "point-person" for my team and any client issues that arise. I am going to meet with my team two days before the workshop to plan for my absence, and meet with them the day after the workshop to ensure any issues that arose during my absence were immediately addressed.

ATTENDING THIS WORKSHOP, AS WELL AS ANY CHALLENGES I FACE MANAGING MY ABSENCE, WILL HELP ME GROW MY CAPABILITIES AS A LEADER AT OUR ORGANIZATION. TO THAT END, I AM ALSO REQUESTING THAT YOU APPROVE PAYING FOR THE WORKSHOP WHICH COSTS $499.00 (LUNCH AND MATERIALS INCLUDED).

I AM EXCITED ABOUT THIS OPPORTUNITY AND WOULD APPRECIATE YOUR SUPPORT. THANK YOU FOR YOUR CONSIDERATION OF THIS REQUEST.

BEST REGARDS,

CARL

Figure 9.2

WHAT ARE THE ROLES I CAN PLAY WHEN ENGAGING WITH INDUSTRY ASSOCIATIONS?

You can engage with an industry association in several ways. In most associations, there is something for everyone, and each of these roles varies in their degree of commitment and complexity, as illustrated in Figure 9.3.

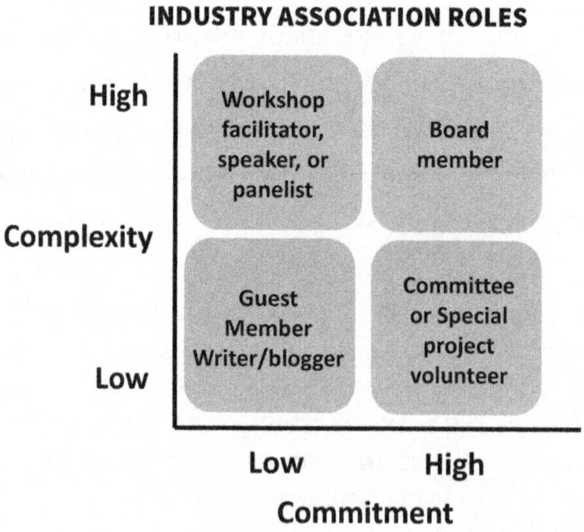

INDUSTRY ASSOCIATION ROLES

Figure 9.3

You can actively engage with an industry association as a:

- **Guest.** Also known affectionately as a "non-member," most association meetings and events are open to everyone. Attending an industry association event before you join the association is a great way to "kick the tires" to assess if this is the group for you.

- **Member.** Once you join the association, you become eligible for the benefits that come with membership, including reduced registration prices for events and access to industry resources that are not open to non-members.

- **Writer/blogger.** Most industry associations have a website, a newsletter, and a blog. If attending a meeting is not possible for you, perhaps providing content for an industry publication is an alternative. Even if you cannot attend every meeting, you can identify a topic of interest to the membership for publication. Industry associations are always seeking content for their newsletters, and your submission will be welcomed.

- **Committee volunteer.** Most associations have a number of committees that allow you to help the association, including finance, marketing, membership, programming, professional development, public relations, and sponsorship. As a volunteer on a committee, you can bring your professional expertise (i.e., your talent with numbers or your love of the sales process) to the association, during the year. Many individuals join a committee before moving on to more complex roles, such as serving on the Board.

- **Special project volunteer**. If participating on a committee for a year feels like too much of a commitment, your industry association may host a special event (e.g., a regional conference) during the year. These special events are like a project – they have a start and end date – and once the event is over, so is your commitment.

- **Workshop/webinar/teleclass facilitator, speaker, or panelist.**
Whether you join your industry association or not, presenting
or participating on a panel is a good way to engage with your
industry. Associations are always looking for speakers who will
elevate the education level of their members.

- **Board of Directors member.** When you are ready to maximize
your visibility within your industry, the Board of Directors is the
place for you. Being on an association board requires the highest
degree of commitment, and represents the highest degree of
complexity. Board roles typically include President, President-
Elect, and Vice-President for the committee roles listed earlier.
Being on a board can be a very rewarding experience, as it provides
you the greatest opportunity to impact member experience.

WHAT ARE THE TYPES OF INDUSTRY ASSOCIATIONS WITH WHICH I CAN ENGAGE?

The types of industry associations that exist are endless. In an effort to create camaraderie among industry professionals, share best practices, provide education, and create opportunity, every industry is represented by numerous associations. Here are some professions and corresponding associations.

If you are a...	Take some time to explore...	At this website address...
Paralegal	The National Federation of Paralegals	paralegals.org
Nurse	The American Nurses Association	nursingworld.org
Product Manager	The Association of International Product Management and Marketing	aipmm.com
Financial Analyst	The Association for Financial Professionals	afponline.org
Quality Administrator	The American Society for Quality	asq.org
Human Resources Manager	The Society for Human Resources Management	shrm.org
Venture Capitalist	The Angel Capital Association	angelcapitalassociation.org
Facilities Manager	The International Facility Management Association	ifma.org
Sales Manager	The Sales Management Association	salesmanagement.org
Electrical Engineer	The Institute of Electrical and Electronics Engineers	ieee.org
Corporate Attorney	The Association of Corporate Counsel	acc.com

Are you looking for associations that represent a specific category rather than a specific job title or industry? Here are some broad categories and an association representing that category:

If you are a...	Take some time to explore...	At this website address...
Graduate of the University of Michigan	The Alumni Association of the University of Michigan	alumni.umich.edu
Female healthcare executive	The Healthcare Businesswomen's Association	hbanet.org
Person from Phoenix, AZ interested in networking	Phoenix Networking and Events	networkingphoenix.com
Black business professional	The Black Business and Professional Organization	bbpa.org
Former employee of Microsoft	The Microsoft Alumni Network	microsoftalumni.com
Person interested in green energy	The Green Collar Association	greencollar.org

If your role, profession, or category is not represented in one of the above tables, simply google your role, profession, or category followed by the word "association." You are bound to find either a local, national, or international association that will provide you an opportunity to engage with individuals who share your interests.

CARL'S DIARY – A POSTSCRIPT

June 17, 2017

"Dear Diary – I finally attended the Software Development Association Monthly meeting last night! It was great to meet so many individuals who do what I do, and understand many of the challenges I face on a daily basis. My strategy to make it to the meeting worked. I told my boss that I wanted to attend the meeting and asked for her support. I mentioned that I wanted to use this time to meet possible candidates for our open Legal Assistant role. We identified critical issues that were pending regarding work on which I have been focused. I asked Marc to be the "point-person" in case any issues came up during my absence. When an urgent issue did arise, my boss went to Marc and they worked it out. I was able to enjoy the meeting and I am planning to join the Membership Committee!"

WHAT ARE SOME WAYS YOU CAN ENGAGE WITH INDUSTRY ASSOCIATIONS?

Here are some typical hurdles to engaging with industry associations and suggestions for improving your level of engagement in your industry.

Engagement Hurdles	Engagement Activities
I do not think belonging to an industry association is a good idea.	• Reach out to one or more colleagues in your functional area or industry, and ask for their experiences and thoughts on the benefits of membership. • Identify a local association that you might consider joining, and contact it to see if you could come to a meeting as a prospective member. • Ask a trusted colleague to challenge your perspective regarding belonging to an industry association to see if you arrive at a different conclusion. Your current perspective may not be accurate, or may no longer be relevant.
I do not belong to an industry association that meets on a recurring basis.	• Join at least one industry association in order to raise your visibility. • Ask several colleagues about associations they are involved in to generate some ideas for you. • Google your functional area along with the words "networking" or "association" to see what groups are in your area. For example, google "accounting associations in Grand Rapids."
I do not participate in presentations or panel discussions at industry association meetings.	• Consider delivering a presentation or participating on a panel at your industry association. Your local groups always need speakers, and they love speakers from within the industry. • Speak with a colleague who has actually made a presentation. Ask about it so that you can gain more information. • Think about possible speaking topics. Chat with a colleague to gauge her reaction to your potential speaking topic. • Participate on a panel discussion to help you eliminate "stage fright." A panel is a great way to talk a limited amount, share the limelight, and practice speaking in front of others.

I do not hold a board role, nor am I on a committee in an industry association.	• Consider becoming a board or committee member for your industry association. • Speak with a fellow member who served on a board or committee. Ask him about his experience to garner useful information. • Take some time to think about roles or committees which interest you the most. Chat with a colleague to gauge his reaction to your ideas. • Ask your industry association about other ways you can help, especially if serving on the board or on a committee is not a good fit for you. Some organizations have one-time events which need extra volunteers.
I do not feel that I have the support of my boss in being a member of an industry association.	• Schedule time with your boss to discuss your interest in joining an industry association group. An ideal time for this conversation is during the budget planning cycle, so you can suggest that the costs of membership and meeting registration can be included in the budget. • Work with a colleague to identify three to five benefits to the organization for joining an industry association, and include this information in your memo or during your conversation with your boss. • Explore if the industry association has "corporate" memberships that allow an organization to join, rather than just one person. This way, other colleagues from your organization can benefit as well.

MY ENGAGE WITH INDUSTRY ASSOCIATIONS ACTIVITY GRID

What are my activities?	How frequently will I perform this activity?	When will I start?	What is my first step?	What risk exists in making progress?	How will I address this risk?

Chapter Nine Recap

- **Engaging with industry associations** is the degree to which you interact and participate with colleagues *outside* of your organization.

- You may not be engaging with industry associations due to a lack of energy, time, information, and support.

- In addition to raising your visibility and value *within* your organization, it is more important than ever to raise your visibility *outside* of your organization as well.

- Maximum visibility resides in a combination of organization *and* industry visibility.

- The percentage of time that you spend cultivating your organization or industry visibility is significantly less important than *cultivating both* in the first place.

- If you are waiting until you need to engage with your industry versus engaging proactively, it is already too late.

- You can engage with your industry for multiple reasons:
  - To identify talent
  - To hear best practices
  - To introduce best practices
  - To meet experts
  - To demonstrate openness

- The best way to minimize your boss's possible perception that you might be joining an industry association to look for a job is to be proactive and engaging with industry associations.

- In order to ensure that your boss's mindset regarding industry association engagement is a hurdle and not a roadblock, follow these steps:

- Be open with your boss
- Ask for support
- Plan for your absence
- Deliver on your plan
- You can engage with an industry association by being a:
  - Guest
  - Member
  - Writer/blogger
  - Committee volunteer
  - Special project volunteer
  - Workshop/webinar/teleclass facilitator, speaker, or panelist
  - Member of a Board of Directors
- The number and types of industry associations are myriad. To find one that fits you, simply google your role, profession, or category followed by the word "association."

CHAPTER TEN

Visibility Accelerator #7
Manage Your Reputation

It seems like just another workday for Carl. As he sits behind his closed door, anchored to his office chair, and wrapped up in his own world, the axis on which his organization turns is spinning furiously. He has not responded to several urgent queries from his colleagues. He decided to skip a morning breakfast being hosted by his organization's new Chief Financial Officer. "Who will miss me?" thought Carl's inner critic as he slinked by the employee cafeteria, praying not to be noticed, and quietly slid into his office. It is likely that he will skip the first meeting of the year for the legal networking group that a colleague suggested he attend that evening. Working to keep his head above water, Carl reaches for his coffee only to find that the steaming hot mocha hazelnut macchiato he purchased a short while ago, similar to his career, has cooled considerably.

Uncharacteristically, Carl decides to leave his office to grab a fresh cup of coffee. As he walks down the hall, he hears his name emanate from a conversation being held in a conference room he is passing. Carl stops to surreptitiously hear what his colleagues are saying.

Colleague #1: "I'm so frustrated! I've asked for the updated brief at least a dozen times and I cannot get Carl to respond. What is it with that guy?"

Colleague #2: "I know how you feel. I needed a simple question answered last month for a case I was working on, and you would think I was asking for a cure for cancer. It was painful just trying to get his attention, let alone an answer."

Colleague #1: "Doesn't he know that he is making all of our lives complicated? I hope Sharon says something to him soon. If she doesn't, I'm just going to go elsewhere when I need some information."

Colleague #2: "I've already starting to bypass him. And it is not just us. Everyone's bypassing him. His reputation is horrible."

Carl is stunned. Is this really how people think and speak about him when he is not around? After all, this isn't how they act when he is present! Moments ago, it seemed like just another workday. Now it feels like a Monday Carl will never forget.

THE IMPORTANCE OF A GOOD REPUTATION

The *Visibility Accelerators* that you have explored thus far are *activities that you do* or *behaviors that you demonstrate* in order to raise your visibility. These accelerators are defined as the behaviors that help you be seen in your organization and industry. Our final *Visibility Accelerator* is focused on the activities and behaviors that help you become known in your organization and industry. These activities and behaviors help build your good reputation.

The importance of having a good reputation is not new. From your early days sitting or kneeling in your house of worship, to Friday night dinners with your grandparents, to lectures in grade school by Girl Scout leaders, you have heard about the importance of a good reputation.

Great minds throughout history have reflected on the importance of a good reputation. These reflections go back thousands of years, people! Here are a few examples:

"The way to gain a good reputation is to endeavor to be what you desire to appear."

- Socrates (470 BC – 399 BC)

"Reputation is an idle and most false impression; oft got without merit, and lost without deserving."

- William Shakespeare (1564 – 1616)

"Associate with men of good quality if you esteem your reputation; for it is better to be alone than in bad company."

- George Washington (1732 – 1799)

"Character is like a tree and reputation like a shadow. The shadow is what we think of it; the tree is the real thing."

- Abraham Lincoln (1809 – 1865)

"You can't build a good reputation on what you are going to do."

- Henry Ford (1863 – 1947)

"It takes twenty years to build a reputation and five minutes to ruin it. If you think about that, you would do things differently."

- Warren Buffett (1930 – present)

WHAT IS NEW ABOUT MANAGING YOUR REPUTATION?

While the importance of a good reputation is not new, the *environment* in which you are working to build a good reputation is. Twenty years ago, your reputation as a business professional was confined to the experiences of individuals with whom you interacted with in your organization or shared experiences with at industry meetings. The relationships with your colleagues were as stable as your work environment – these were the same folks you had been working with or had known for years. Perhaps your reputation expanded outside of your cloistered circle of colleagues when you spoke at a national industry event or published an article or research paper. Beyond that, few individuals knew who you were, let alone had an opinion about your reputation.

Today, chaos and change rule the day. The frequency and pace of change defines the "new normal" in corporations around the globe. Your ability to build strong relationships over time is becoming harder. The individuals with whom you worked yesterday are gone today. Lines of responsibility are blurring. The number of new people with whom you come in contact, both physically and virtually, is growing weekly.

At the same time, you are changing faster than ever. In their book, *The Start-Up of You,* authors Reid Hoffman and Ben Casnocha suggest that you need to always be in "beta" mode in order to survive and succeed in today's fast-paced and frenetic corporate environments. They encourage you to "think of yourself as a work-in-progress" and "invest in yourself every single day."[1] These never-ending and fast-paced changes define the professional environments you find yourself in today. However, always being in "beta" creates its own set of challenges. Recurring ways in which you change in the midst of fast-changing environments create risk to your reputation, as illustrated in Figure 10.1.

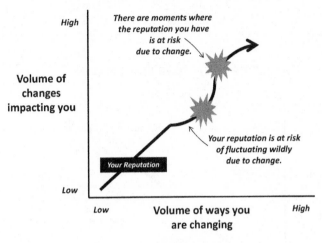

Figure 10.1

Imagine a situation where you are attempting to be a "work-in-progress" in an environment that is always changing. It's like learning to play golf in the midst of a hurricane. Learning to play golf is hard, even on a beautiful day. Surviving a hurricane is hard, even with tremendous preparation. Mesh golf lessons (always being in "beta") and a hurricane (your fast-changing environment) together and chaos will reign.

At the same time, the proliferation of professional transparency is creating new ways for individuals to develop an opinion about you. You can now share information about yourself in endless ways (e.g., Facebook, LinkedIn, Twitter, blogging), most of which do not even require you to be physically present. Individuals that you have never met and may never meet can find information about you faster than the time it took you to read this sentence.

As illustrated in Figure 10.2, the nexus of the growth in the ways that you can share information about yourself and the number of opinions that can be developed about you is exploding. While you are working your life away in Dubuque, Iowa, a colleague from another city is reading a blog you wrote. While you are snoring away in Jakarta, India, someone in another time zone is taking a peek at your Facebook page. While you are stuck in another late night meeting in Paris, France, wondering, "What am I doing here?" a recruiter is starting his day by reading your LinkedIn profile.

THE NEXUS OF SHARING AND OPINION

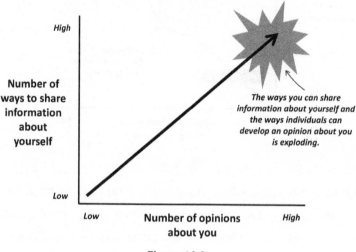

Figure 10.2

Unless you are Superman or Superwoman, you cannot be everywhere at once. In your absence, at some point during the day, someone is thinking and speaking about you. Perhaps you finished a presentation and a few of your colleagues stayed behind to chat about next steps. In the midst of that conversation, comments about you surface. Perhaps a group of senior executives are discussing candidates to fill a key vacancy in the organization and you are one of those candidates. Perhaps you are on your way to get a cup of coffee and you hear colleagues speaking about you in a conference room. This "echo" of you that exists in the thoughts and words of your colleagues is your reputation.

REPUTATION IS HOW YOUR COLLEAGUES THINK OR SPEAK ABOUT YOU WHEN YOU ARE NOT PRESENT.

CAN I CHOOSE MY REPUTATION OR IS MY REPUTATION CHOSEN FOR ME BY OTHERS?

The work that I do with my leadership coaching clients often focuses on the power of choice. My clients like talking about the concept of choice as they aspire to be more focused in what they choose to do and how they choose to do it. Often, however, in situations where my clients do have a choice, they erroneously believe they have no choice.

There are certainly things you cannot choose. You can't choose not to get multiple sclerosis. You can't choose to win a million dollars in a lottery. You can't choose someone to love you. However, if you were to list all of the experiences in your life and weigh each of them equally, you would find over 98% of these experiences resulted from a choice you made. I am not diminishing the importance of the remaining 2% - I am merely pointing out the number of choices you can make.

At first, you probably do not feel that 98% of your activities are the result of a choice. This is because you do not realize how many choices you make every day. Whether it is to hit the snooze button on your alarm clock a third time, to brush your teeth before you take a shower, or have one packet of Splenda in your coffee rather than two, by the time you leave your home, you are a choice-making machine.

You make so many choices, you may not even realize that some things that you did today were a choice. Or you may believe that a decision you made today was not up to you. Many of my clients find themselves in a state commonly called "victim mode." They believe that the outcome to a situation in which they had a voice was not up to them. They believe they "had no choice." When you are in victim mode, you will say something similar to one of the following, usually in a defensive tone:

- "I had to miss the meeting. I had no choice."
- "I had to fire Sue. What was I supposed to do?"
- "We don't have a choice on this. We need to pick Option A and move on."

When you are in "victim mode," you abdicate your ability to make a choice. Perhaps you are abdicating your choice to another person. Perhaps you are just "going along" with someone else's decision. Perhaps you are protecting your need for status, self-worth, and contribution. Whatever your reason, you believe that you *did not* have a choice when, in fact, *you did* have a choice.

WHAT INFLUENCES A REPUTATION?

Your reputation is built on a never-ending series of choices that you make every day. And in today's transparent and frenetic organizations, your choices are seen by more of your colleagues, and faster than ever before.

Today's ever-changing organizations demand that you be in charge of your reputation. Every Facebook post you choose to generate, sound bite you choose to create, and decision you choose to make will potentially be seen or heard by thousands of colleagues in your organization and industry. Your choices are your reputation. In my work with my clients and throughout my career, I have observed that reputations are influenced by four areas – **articulation, attitude, behavior,** and **production,** as illustrated in Figure 10.3.

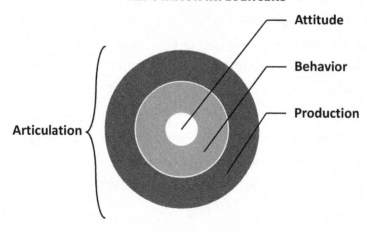

Figure 10.3

ARTICULATION

When it comes to your reputation, your colleagues are going to *think* what they want to think and *say* what they want to say. Since the reputation you have exists in the thoughts and words of your colleagues (especially when you are not present), the focus of your time and energy is to *influence* those thoughts and words, as illustrated in Figure 10.4.

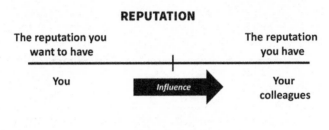

Figure 10.4

The first step to identifying the reputation you want to have begins with your ability to **articulate** it. If you can't describe your reputation yourself, you can't expect others to think and speak about you in the ways that you want them to think and speak about you. It would be like driving from New York City to San Francisco without knowing how to get there. *Who knows where you will end up?* It would be like walking into a theater to watch a movie without knowing what movie you are about to see. *Who knows if you will like it or not?* It would be like asking your accountant to complete your taxes, without knowing the outcome. *Who knows if the outcome is right or wrong?*

If you want people to think about you and describe you in a positive way when you are not present, you need to be the first one to articulate your reputation the way you would want others to articulate it.

ARTICULATION IS THE DEGREE TO WHICH YOU CAN DESCRIBE
THE GOOD REPUTATION YOU WANT TO HAVE.

Let's get started. Take a moment to think about the reputation you want to exist in the thoughts and words of your colleagues, and write this reputation in the box below.

> THE REPUTATION *I* WANT TO HAVE IS ARTICULATED AS FOLLOWS
>
> _____
>
> _____

You may have found it easy to write down the reputation you want to have. You may have spent a long time writing a response, perhaps erasing your first few attempts to do so. Maybe you scratched out a few words, replaced them with new ones, scratched out the new words, and repeated the cycle.

Crafting a reputation statement is not easy. When was the last time you took a few moments to think about the reputation you want to have? How do you know if the choices you are making support the reputation you want to have? If you are like the majority of busy business professionals with whom I work, you have never spent time seriously thinking about the reputation you want to have. You have never spent time considering the importance of influencing the thoughts and words of your colleagues when they speak about you when you are not present. No doubt you have expected that your "nose-to-the-grindstone" work ethic would ensure rapturous thoughts and words about you after you have left the room.

Before finalizing your reputation statement, consider the following additional areas which influence your reputation. We will come back and revisit how to craft an effective reputation statement later in this chapter.

ATTITUDE

Attitude is one of those human characteristics that is very hard to describe. If you were to ask the next colleague you see to define the word "attitude," you will likely be met by a blank stare or a fumbling response. Attitude seems to have a million definitions. How about you? Take a moment to think about and jot down your definition of attitude.

ATTITUDE IS _____

_____

_____

If you are similar to most of your colleagues, defining attitude was not quick and intuitive. Many of you will avoid trying to describe attitude and simply say, "I know it when I see it." You don't think a lot about the definition of attitude until you are asked to share an opinion regarding a colleague. As you think about your colleague, one of the defining characteristics on which you will reflect is his attitude. It is very common to hear something similar to one of the following statements when you are thinking about one of your colleagues:

- "I love Carol! She has a great attitude and always gets her work done with a smile."
- "David? Ugh! That guy has such a bad attitude. I stay away from him as much as I can."
- "Mark is a real go-to guy. I can really depend on him to deliver."

Humans are attuned to attitude whether you are perceived by your colleagues as having a good or bad one. While attitude is hard to define, your colleagues definitely will "know it when they see it."

> Your **ATTITUDE** IS COMPRISED OF THE *INTANGIBLE* CHOICES YOU MAKE TO BUILD YOUR GOOD REPUTATION.

As our focus is on building a good reputation, it is natural that our focus will also be on a good attitude. A good attitude is typically reflected by the following attributes:

- **Optimism**. You choose to be positive and have a "can-do" perspective.

- **Flexibility**. You choose to be open to change and generous in the number of options that you are willing to consider.

- **Politeness**. You choose to be kind and courteous to your colleagues, even during times of stress and conflict.

BEHAVIOR

If attitude reflects the *intangible* choices that you make regarding people and situations, **behavior** reflects the *tangible* choices you make which influence your reputation.

Behavior is easier to define than attitude, as we can see behavior more readily. While you can see some aspects of attitude (i.e., a smile on an optimistic colleague or a look of exasperation by a negative co-worker), behavior is where the "rubber hits the road."

> Your **BEHAVIOR** IS COMPRISED OF THE *TANGIBLE* CHOICES YOU MAKE TO BUILD YOUR GOOD REPUTATION.

Behavioral psychologists suggest that if you want to know what a person is thinking, watch their behavior. Dr. Carl Jung, a noted psychologist, is quoted as saying, "You are what you do, not what you say you will do.²" More colloquially, you are familiar with the idioms, "Actions speaks louder than words" and "I'll believe it when I see it." Your daughter can promise you "six ways to sundown" that she will be home by 11:00 pm. Did she get home by 11:00 pm or did she provide you a litany of reasons as to why she was delayed? Did her actions speak louder than her words? Your state senator can insert every sound bite in his intention to vote "no" for a bill coming up for consideration. Did he vote "no," or did a last minute epiphany change his decision to a "yes" vote? Did his actions speak louder than his words?

Every day you make behavioral choices that help or hurt your reputation. Behavior is what people hear or see when interacting with you and is comprised of the following two activities:

- **What you say.** Your behavior is defined by what, when, and how you *say* something.

- **What you do.** Your behavior is defined by what, when, and how you *do* something.

While "what you say" and "what you do" are independently important, how these activities relate to one another cannot be overstated. At the intersection between what you say and what you do is **integrity,** the most important characteristic of a good reputation.

THE FOUNDATION FOR INTEGRITY

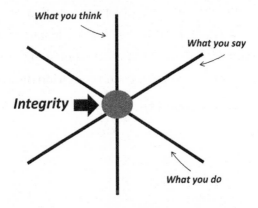

Figure 10.5

Numerous books and articles have been written focusing on the importance of integrity. College courses offer analyses of integrity, and professors integrate examples from the past, as well as the present. The idea of integrity as the foundation to a good reputation is an idea as old as reputation itself. *Merriam Webster's Dictionary* provides a number of synonyms for integrity, such as "character," "decency," "goodness," "honesty," "morality," "probity," "rectitude," "righteousness," "virtue," and "virtuousness." In the *Raise Your Visibility & Value* model, when you operate with integrity you give your reputation a strong foundation upon which to build. However you define it, integrity exists when "*what you say*" and "*what you do*" are aligned.

It is important to acknowledge that another component of integrity is "how you think." True integrity exists at the intersection of how you think about something, what you say about it, and how you behave in relation to it, as illustrated in Figure 10.5. Since "how you think" is less behaviorally based, I will not be spending time in the area of thinking as it relates to integrity and reputation. I do want to influence, however, how you think about the idea of raising your visibility in your organization and industry. My goal is to ensure that your behavior is consistent when you work to build a good reputation.

When "what you say" and "what you do" are not aligned, like a space invasion video arcade game from the 1980's, your ability to operate with integrity comes under attack. As illustrated in Figure 10.6, it becomes impossible to build a good reputation. Your colleagues see your behavior as scattershot. You are "all over the place," behaving inconsistently and without integrity. Your hope for a good reputation dissipates.

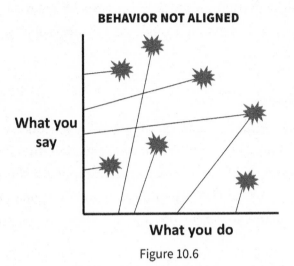

Figure 10.6

When "what you say" and "what you do" are aligned, your colleagues will see you as a person who operates with integrity. Your colleagues will think or say, "She does what she says she will do." Your integrity is aligned and it acts as a strong foundation for a good reputation, as illustrated in Figure 10.7.

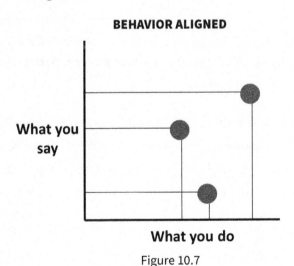

Figure 10.7

All of the prior *Visibility Accelerators* - how you introduce yourself, how you create accessibility, how responsive you are, how you interact and participate with others, and how you engage in industry associations

- provide you with opportunities to act with integrity, choose behaviors that build your good reputation, and raise your visibility in your organization and industry.

PRODUCTION

Having a good attitude, demonstrating good behaviors, and acting with integrity are only part of the reputation equation. In today's fast-paced organizations, it is almost assumed that the work you produce is good. Even colleagues who demonstrate a good attitude and good behaviors may find themselves in job jeopardy if they are not producing good work.

Production is comprised of the following categories:

- **Quantity.** The *volume* of work that you do meets or exceeds the expectations of those for whom the work is being produced.

- **Quality.** The *nature* of work that you do meets or exceeds the expectations of those for whom the work is being produced.

> **PRODUCTION** REFLECTS THE QUANTITY AND QUALITY OF WORK THAT YOU DO TO BUILD YOUR GOOD REPUTATION.

It should not be surprising to you that doing what you do with a high degree of quantity and quality is an important part of a good reputation. Quantity and quality are similar to what you say and do in that quantity and quality need to be in balance. When quantity and quality are not in balance, the impact to your reputation is not positive, as illustrated in Figure 10.8.

THE IMPACT OF PRODUCTION ON REPUTATION

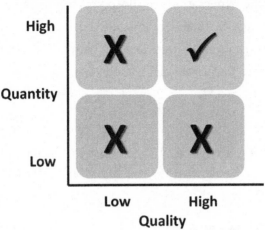

Figure 10.8

- **Low Quantity + Low Quality.** Face it! If you produce a low quantity of work and the work you do produce is low quality, your days are numbered. Even the best attitude and behavior will not offset low quantity and poor quality. Your hopes of being chosen as Employee of the Quarter are slim.

- **Low Quantity + High Quality.** Good news! The work you are producing is of high quality. The bad news is that there is too little of it. It helps that you have a good attitude and that you demonstrate good behavior, yet this will only take you so far. If you could just grow your volume of work without diminishing quality, your dream of being chosen as Employee of the Quarter could become a reality.

- **High Quantity + Low Quality.** Congratulations! You have a great reputation as a workhorse. You produce more work than all of your colleagues combined. Unfortunately, the quality of your work is so low it seems more like you are horsing around. Your hopes of being chosen as Employer of the Quarter will be met – just at another company.

- **High Quantity + High Quality.** Eureka! You are meeting or exceeding the expectations of those for whom you are producing work. Your quantity is where it should be and your work is of high quality. Your reputation in respect to the work that you produce is also high. The Employee of the Quarter plaque has already been engraved!

WHEN YOU CONSIDER THE FOUR AREAS HIGHLIGHTED ABOVE, WHICH OF THE FOUR AREAS DESCRIBE YOU THE BEST?

A NOTE ON QUALITY

Quality is in the eye of the beholder. In order to influence the "beholder," there are some key behaviors that help ensure that you distinguish yourself amongst your colleagues. Most of your colleagues would consider that quality exists when work is done with the highest degree of excellence. Consider the following behaviors to help you achieve a high degree of excellence:

- **Set expectations.** Be clear about the nature of the work and how and when it will be completed.

- **Be timely.** Complete your work consistent with the expectations that have been set as to when the work would be completed.

- **Communicate changes proactively.** Update stakeholders as quickly as possible to identify a change in the expectations you have previously communicated.

- **Reset expectations.** If changes arise that impact your ability to meet the expectations you have previously communicated, reset the expectations.

ARTICULATION REVISITED

Now that you have digested the influencers of a good reputation – attitude, behavior, and production - it is time to revisit the reputation statement you crafted earlier in the chapter to determine if there is an opportunity to improve it.

In the *Raise Your Visibility & Value* model, a reputation statement is comprised of the following components:

Reputation = Attitude + Behavior + Production

These components act as the architecture of a reputation statement that you can articulate and utilize as the foundation for your good reputation. In order to help you get started, here are some words, in Figure 10.9, that describe attitudes and behaviors that comprise a good reputation:

WORDS THAT DESCRIBE A GOOD REPUTATION

✓	I want to be described as:	Which means I...
	Achieving	Accomplish increasingly challenging goals on a regular basis.
	Active	Take action and I am always on the go.
	Analytical	Conduct detailed examinations for purposes of definition and understanding.
	Articulate	Speak with clear and precise words and phrases.
	Conscientious	Act with extreme care and attentiveness.
	Courageous	Persevere through danger, pain, or difficulty.
	Creative	Generate new associations for ideas and concepts.
	Curious	Learn eagerly.
	Decisive	Reach a decision quickly, firmly, and clearly.
	Diligent	Perform tasks quietly and steadily to a high degree of exactness.

✓	I want to be described as:	Which means I...
	Diplomatic	Handle difficult matters with courtesy and empathy in an effort to minimize harm.
	Disciplined	Follow a process or rule to achieve a consistent outcome.
	Empathetic	Recognize and understand another's state of mind or emotion.
	Enthusiastic	Show great excitement and interest.
	Flexible	Adjust readily to different conditions.
	Focused	Concentrate energy on an identified problem or goal.
	Generous	Give without limit or coercion.
	Honest	Speak and act truthfully.
	Humorous	Provoke laughter and provide amusement.
	Possessing Integrity	Illustrate consistent values and actions.
	Independent	Act freely from external control or constraint.
	Kind	Possess a considerate and helpful nature.
	Loyal	Give support to a person or a cause.
	Observant	Pay close attention and quick to notice details.
	Open-minded	Weigh new and different ideas and opinions.
	Optimistic	Expect the best in all possible ways.
	Organized	Interact with the world in a methodical and structured way.
	Passionate	Have and express strong feelings.
	Patient	Endure trying circumstances with an even temper.
	Persistent	Achieve an outcome.
	Persuasive	Induce others to adopt an action or a belief.
	Resourceful	Use available resources wisely or ingeniously.
	Strategic	Think broadly and long-term, often in areas of complexity.
	Supportive	Provide positive assistance and encouragement.
	Wise	Exercise good judgment and common sense in practical matters.
	Add Your Own	
	Add Your Own	
	Add Your Own	
	Add Your Own	

Figure 10.9

Using our formula for building a reputation statement and some of the words that describe a good attitude and good behavior, peruse this reputation statement:

"I want to be known as optimistic and flexible. I want to expect the best in everything that I do and adjust readily to varying conditions. I want to demonstrate behaviors associated with being resourceful and decisive. I want to produce a high volume of work that is known for its quality."

Take a moment to revisit the reputation statement you crafted earlier. If you feel it can be improved, rewrite your new reputation statement below, focusing on attitude, behavior, and production.

THE REPUTATION I WANT TO HAVE CAN BE ARTICULATED AS FOLLOWS

_____

_____

_____

A GOOD REPUTATION DOES NOT EQUAL PERFECTION!

Building and maintaining a good reputation takes a lot of hard work. When you utilize the *Visibility Accelerators* we have discussed, your likelihood of reducing risk and increasing opportunity grows. In the midst of all your efforts, give yourself permission to be imperfect. Being perfect is too high a pedestal on which any of us should stand. Rest assured that your good reputation comes from being human, not from being perfect.

What are Some Ways You Can Manage Your Reputation?

Here are some typical hurdles to managing your reputation and suggestions for managing your reputation in your organization and industry.

Reputation Hurdles	Reputation Activities
I do not demonstrate a positive attitude with my confidential "inner circle" (work friends with whom I can share anything).	• Read a book (e.g., Norman Vincent Peale's *The Power of Positive Thinking*) or an article about building and illustrating a positive attitude. From your reading, identify two or three activities you can do to make progress in building a more positive attitude. • Ask for feedback from one or more trusted colleagues on your attitude at work. Give your colleagues permission to be candid in the spirit of helping you become more effective. • Observe your behavior during your next interaction with your "inner circle." Refrain from comments that could be perceived as negative. • Create a goal to focus only on the positive when you are with your "inner circle." Watch for how much positive conversation is occurring and remember how easy it is to get persuaded to negative conversations.
I do not know the reputation I have in my organization.	• Partner with your manager or your Human Resources business partner on ways in which you can gain greater insight into your reputation at work. • Contact your organization's Leadership Development department to see if your organization uses an assessment that would help you understand your reputation. • Contact a trusted colleague (at work or elsewhere) with whom you can have a candid conversation on what colleagues may say about you when you are not around. Work on ways to further illustrate the positive observations and improve the negative observations.

Reputation Hurdles	Reputation Activities
I do not think I have a positive reputation in my organization.	• Partner with your manager or your Human Resources business partner on ways in which you can improve your reputation at work. • Read a book (e.g., *How to Build Your Reputation* by Rob Brown) or an article about reputation management. • Identify a colleague whom you believe possesses a positive reputation. Schedule a time with her to talk about your efforts to improve your reputation. Ask her for her ideas on how to have a positive reputation. • Craft a new reputation statement and begin to focus on your attitude, behaviors, and production. It is never too late to build a good reputation.
I can be perceived by my colleagues as having a negative attitude.	• Partner with your manager on ways in which you can improve your attitude at work. A perception of having a negative attitude at work is not a good foundation upon which to build your visibility. • Work with a career coach who can help you explore the originations of your negative attitude and create strategies to improve your attitude. • Read a book (e.g., *Success Through a Positive Mental Attitude* by Napoleon Hill) or an article on improving a negative attitude. • Take some "you" time to think about how you can improve your attitude. Sometimes a break from work can help improve a negative attitude or the perception of one.
I cannot articulate the reputation I have in my organization.	• Partner with your manager, your Human Resources business partner, or a career coach on ways in which you can articulate and create more visibility around your reputation at work. • Create a reputation statement that can act as the foundation for the reputation you wish to have and articulate that statement.

MY *MANAGE YOUR REPUTATION* ACTIVITY GRID

What are my activities?	How frequently will I perform this activity?	When will I start?	What is my first step?	What risk exists in making progress?	How will I address this risk?

Chapter Ten Recap

- **Reputation** is how your colleagues think or speak about you when you are not present.

- Reputation is focused on the activities and behaviors that help you **be known** in your organization and industry.

- The importance of a good reputation has been around for thousands of years. While the *importance* of a reputation is not new, the *environment* in which you are working to build a reputation is new.

- Recurring change in how you are building your reputation in the midst of fast-changing environments creates risk to your reputation.

- When you work to raise your visibility and value in your organization and industry, your goal is to make choices that build a *good* reputation.

- Colleagues are influenced by the following four areas when thinking about their own or a colleague's reputation:

  - **Articulation** is the degree to which you can describe the good reputation you want to have and is the first step in defining this desired reputation.

  - **Attitude** is comprised of the *intangible* choices you make regarding your good reputation.

  - **Behavior** is comprised of the *tangible* choices you make to build your good reputation.

  - **Production** reflects the quantity and quality of the work that you do to build your good reputation.

- **Integrity** exists when what you say and what you do are aligned.

- **Quality** is achieved by doing the following:

- Set expectations
- Be timely
- Communicate changes proactively
- Reset expectations

- You can create the reputation you want by creating a **reputation statement,** which is a combination of attitude, behavior, and production.

- Having a good reputation does not mean you have to be perfect. Give yourself permission to be human and imperfect.

PART THREE

Raise Your Value

Chapter Eleven

Raise Your Value

"Try not to become a person of success,
but rather try to become a person of value."
Albert Einstein

Now that you have read about the first part of the *Raise Your Visibility & Value* formula – **visibility** – let's delve deeper into the second part of the equation – **value.**

Every once in a while, you will hear the Chief Executive Officer of an organization declare "At Acme Products, we are like a family!" I am not sure what a CEO means when she describes her company as a family. Does everyone at the company sit down for dinner on Sunday evening? Does everyone share a hotel room while vacationing at the Grand Canyon? And who keeps leaving the refrigerator door open?

Perhaps there was a time when organizations were familial. Your grandparents may reminisce about the "good old days" when employees were treated like family. In the not-too-distant past, family-like environments naturally flourished since the frequency and pace of change was slower, tenures were longer, and relationships were deeper. Doing your job well was tantamount to a guarantee of lifetime employment.

However, organizations today *are not* like a family, regardless of what your well-intentioned CEO tells you. In functional families, "blood is thicker than water," and family always comes first. Whether you are a mother, step-father, sister, brother-in-law, aunt, uncle, beloved or estranged, you are and will always be historically, legally or genetically a family member.

Conversely, in most organizations, the organization always comes first. While business is on the upswing, your relationship with your employer will flourish. Moods are positive and opportunities are abundant. Hope springs eternal! Yet, it is the belief that good times are forever, and that relationships will supercede a tough decision that leaves most business professionals surprised, shocked, and hurt. When red ink starts to rise as financials tighten or competition heats up, reorganizations, restructurings, and reductions rule the day. Good performers are suddenly reminded that they are liabilities on a balance sheet and liabilities must be reduced in order to stabilize financials. "Family members" are suddenly and unceremoniously asked to pack-up their belongings and exit the building, escorted to the door by Harold from Security. In organizations, blood is not thicker than water – red ink is.

Allyn Gardner, the long-time career coach at Harvard Business School's career program for MBA students, has observed this phenomenon first hand. "They call people human capital for a reason," Allyn mused. "Capital is an asset that you review periodically to determine how well it is performing to meet your objectives. Businesses tend to focus more on the capital-side and less on the human-side."

In 2009, Netflix published a culture manifesto called the *"Netflix Culture: Freedom and Responsibility."*[1] This 126-slide PowerPoint behemoth is segmented into the *Seven Aspects of Our Culture*, designed to clarify Netflix's view of how it measures professional success. Embedded in this manifesto is a slide (Figure 11.1) that reads:

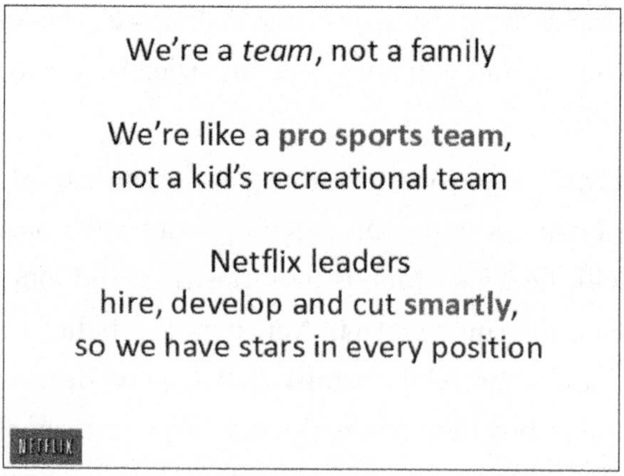

We're a *team*, not a family

We're like a **pro sports team**,
not a kid's recreational team

Netflix leaders
hire, develop and cut **smartly**,
so we have stars in every position

Figure 11.1

Notice how "cut" is given equal weight as "hire" and "develop." While "cutting" a colleague is never enjoyable, it is becoming as natural an activity in your organization as saying "good morning" to a colleague at the Keurig coffee maker in your break area.

In today's "get-it-done-yesterday" business environments, the frequency and pace of change is accelerating, tenure is shortening, and relationships are becoming shallower. Herminia Ibarra, the Cora Chaired Professor of Leadership and Professor of Organizational Behavior at Institut Européen d'Administration des Affaires (INSEAD), reflected on this topic in a recent *Wall Street Journal* article. "With competition fierce and the business climate changing rapidly, companies are telling their leaders that it's no longer enough to deliver results in their individual departments, or over the short-term."[2] Doing your job well, which often results in an "exceeds expectations" rating on your annual performance appraisal, is no longer enough. You must do more than just do your job well.

You must go beyond providing good performance. You must create value for your organization. While your organization's balance sheet might classify you as a liability, you must act like an asset. And, like most assets, the value you create needs to appreciate over time. If you are not viewed as valuable, you are at risk, similar to any underperforming asset, of being divested and escorted out of the building.

WHAT IS VALUE?

In order to have a conversation regarding raising your value in your organization, we need to have a common definition of value from which to work. In the *Raise Your Visibility & Value* model:

> **VALUE** IS WHEN THE OUTCOME OF A SITUATION EXCEEDS
> THE COST INCURRED BY A SATISFACTORY MARGIN.

While most of the words and phrases in this definition are self-explanatory, "outcome of a situation," "cost," and "satisfactory margin" require additional explanation:

- **Outcome of a situation.** How you assess value starts with the outcome you are seeking in the first place. Another way to think about this is to ask yourself, "What are my expectations for an outcome?" Expectations play a significant role in how you feel about the outcome of a situation into which you are entering. Expectations frame the amount of value we are looking to receive. Even if a pound of bananas is on sale at your local grocery store, if it is still higher than what you thought it would be, you will likely feel as though the value you are receiving is low – in other words, the value is not meeting your expectations. Here is another example: You may be expecting a certain amount of money for your raise this year. Even if the amount of your raise is competitive in the marketplace and higher than your peers, if the amount is below your expectations. You will likely feel bad about the outcome of the situation. When something meets your expectations, you generally feel good. When something does not meet your expectations, you generally do not feel good. Understanding what your expectations are for the outcome of a situation and understanding the expectations of others for the outcome of a situation play an important role in the perception of value creation.

- **Cost.** When you read or hear the word "cost," you typically think about money. Questions and statements such as "How much is that going to cost?" and "That costs too much!" are likely to pop into your head. However, costs are more than just money. As a busy business professional in a fast-moving workplace, you manage several assets that become costs when you use them. When it comes to understanding value, these assets are time, energy, and money, as illustrated in Figure 11.2.

TYPES OF COST

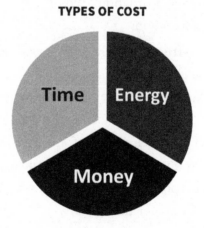

Figure 11.2

- **Time.** Your time is valuable. You do not have enough time in your day to accomplish all that you want to accomplish, so how you invest your time is very important. You have grown up hearing phrases like "Time is money!" You can still hear Fred Flintstone's boss, Mr. Slate, yelling "FLINTSTONE!" and George Jetson's boss, Mr. Spacely, yelling "JETSON!" when productivity did not meet their expectations. Feeling as though your time is well-spent to receive a benefit by a satisfactory margin enhances the potential for value. Feeling as though an activity is a waste of your time indicates an absence of value - the cost of the outcome was greater than the benefit.

- **Energy.** As a human being, you only have so much energy to expend. While you may have more (or less) energy than a colleague, regardless of how much energy you have, your energy only goes so far. Energy is very present in our lives. You may describe yourself as a "morning person" because your energy is low by the time the afternoon kicks-in. You may occasionally think to yourself "I don't have the energy for this" because you are already juggling more projects than you can handle. The consumer marketplace knows all about the importance of maintaining your energy level. Products like Red Bull and the Five-Hour Energy Drink are all designed to "boost your energy." Feeling as though the energy you invest is well spent enhances the likelihood for value. Feeling as though you don't have the energy for an activity or that your investment "drains your energy" indicates that the cost of an outcome is or was greater than its benefit.

- **Money.** While there are other types of financial assets in the world, when you think about costs, you probably think in a monetary context. If you are going to invest your hard-earned money in something, you will always want to receive a benefit that exceeds the cost. This is also true when you are spending someone else's money, such as your organization's money. This correlation between money and value is where value shows up most often in our culture. McDonald's "Value Menu" and Walmart's "Value of the Day" are commonplace in our lexicon. Businesses across the globe bombard us with sales pitches that imply the benefits of spending your money on their products and services, significantly outweighing the costs incurred.

These three assets – time, energy, and money - are interdependent. For example, you could have all the time and energy in the world, yet you are unable to invest in a desired outcome, as you do not have the money. Or, you may have the energy and money to invest in your outcome, yet you have little time to make it happen.

- **Satisfactory margin.** Margin is the difference between the amount of cost incurred and the benefit derived. Not all margins, however, are created equal. In order to experience value, the margin must also be satisfactory. For example, a manufacturer produces an item that costs him $10.00 and sells the same item for $12.00; hence, this item has a 20% margin (($12.00 - $10.00) / $10.00). This manufacturer may be very happy with this margin. Yet for another manufacturer, and for a variety of reasons, this margin may be woefully deficient. The point here is not to determine the correct margin for this example, but to recognize that, in order to feel that you are receiving value, you need to feel that the difference between incurred costs and derived benefit is satisfactory. In the workplace, what might be valuable to you may be less so to the person in the office next to you. Value, like beauty, is in the eye of the beholder.

Hence, as you enter into an activity that will provide a benefit, knowing what a satisfactory margin will be in relation to your investment of time, energy, and money is very important to know up front.

WHAT IS RAISING YOUR VALUE?

In the *Raise Your Visibility & Value* model, **raising your value** is defined as follows:

> YOU **RAISE YOUR VALUE** WITH ACTIVITIES THAT CONNECT INDIVIDUAL CONTRIBUTIONS WITH BUSINESS PERFORMANCE.

Similar to most of your colleagues, you spend little time raising your value. You are more likely trapped at your desk working hard to be a good performer and deliver what is expected of you, as defined by your boss or your job description. Your boss's environment does not allow her to focus on value creation, and most job descriptions do not identify ways that your role can create value for your organization. Take a moment to look at your job description. Does it explicitly identify ways that your individual contributions connect with business performance? Are the ways that your organization creates value for its employees, customers, investors, and stockholders identified? If your job description is similar to most other job descriptions, there is no mention of value. The ways to create value are not clear, the metrics to measure value are not stated, and the semantics are not value-focused.

VALUE IS THE NEW CORPORATE CURRENCY!

The head-spinning advances in technology, endless bottom-line financial pressures, and growing networks of global economies described earlier demand a need for superior performance and sustainable efficiencies. Organizations aspire to motivate their employees to be better, more productive, and more engaged. Leaders seek ways to create a common language behind which organizational goals and activities can align. What can replace the void that is being created by the slow demise of performance management systems?

The answer is **value creation.** The language being used to define success is slowly and quietly shifting from *performance* to *value*. If you listen, you can hear "value creation" everywhere. I've been listening. I hear recruiters talk about the importance of creating value. As one recruiter said at a panel I attended, "Don't tell me what you did. Tell me the value you created for your employer. Tell me how _you_ made a difference." I hear entrepreneurs talk about ensuring the products and services they work to bring to market create value in ways that don't currently exist. At my Apple iPhone orientation, an Apple employee enthusiastically espoused that "the thousands of apps that you will now have access to will add value to your life." The good performance of the iPhone was assumed – it was the *value* of the apps that excited him.

How does value exist within your organization? Has a conversation about value begun? Does your organization realize it has overinvested in performance management and underinvested in value creation? Whatever your situation, *value is the new corporate currency*. It is the vehicle upon which the exchange between individual contributions and organizational rewards is occurring. Slowly and quietly, numerical and bell curve-based performance management systems are being shipped to the scrap heap as business leaders seek robust and meaningful ways to increase individual contributions.

Measuring the value that you create for your organization is gaining your boss's attention. Why? Value requires a foundation of good performance, ties your performance to business objectives and financial metrics, and creates a new way to motivate and align you in ways that are more rewarding for everyone involved.

WHAT IS A VALUABLE EMPLOYEE?

When I assert that you must achieve more than just doing your job well, I am not suggesting that doing your job well is not important. Conversely, in today's excruciating work environments, good performance *is expected.* Your organization is finding less time and spending less money to train you to be a good performer. In her recent *Wall Street Journal* article, Herminia Ibarra of INSEAD continued to reflect that "Businesses are putting managers in a tough spot: They're forcing bosses to take on many new responsibilities – but they're not training them to get those jobs done."[3]

At the same time, your organization is spending more time and money finding the "right fit" for your organization under the premise that good performance is a given. Organizations like Zappo's will pay you several thousand dollars to leave if you feel you are not a good fit. Not a good fit at Netflix? You are cut. These organizations at the leading edge of their respective industries would rather pay you to leave than invest in you to fit. Good performance no longer stands alone as a strategy to differentiate you from your colleagues. In order to be a valuable employee, you must be a good performer _and_ an individual whose activities create value for your organization, as illustrated in Figure 11.3.

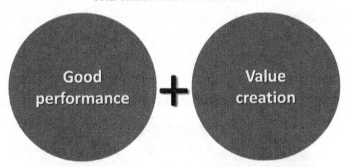

Figure 11.3

WHAT IS GOOD PERFORMANCE?

While it is inevitable that the dreaded performance appraisal as the sole measurement of your contributions to your organization will cease to exist in its current format (insert golf clap), some form of performance measurement will continue to exist. One reason is that roles within organizations where value creation falls into a category called "individual value" (more on types of value in Chapter 12) will need a performance management system to measure how foundational activities impact the organization.

In the _Raise Your Visibility & Value_ model, **good performance** is focused on:

ATTITUDE, BEHAVIOR, AND PRODUCTION

Good performance is focused on the mechanics of how you do your job as organizations work to contrast good performance from value creation. And the good news is that you do not have to look far to understand what these mechanics are, as you have already read about them earlier in this book. Care to hazard a guess where you first saw the mechanics for measuring how you do your job?

Take a moment to flip the pages of this book back to Chapter 10 and look for the section entitled "What Influences a Reputation?" That's right! The same influencers that characterize a good reputation - **attitude, behavior, and production** - are also the same influencers of good performance. Reputation and performance hold a very special relationship in your workplace, as illustrated in Figure 11.4.

THE RELATIONSHIP BETWEEN PERFORMANCE AND REPUTATION

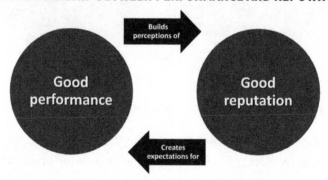

Figure 11.4

Good performance builds the perception your colleagues have of you, creating the foundation of your good reputation. As you demonstrate a positive attitude, helpful behavior, and high production, word spreads about you. The ways your colleagues talk about you when you are not in the room is positive and constructive. Concurrently, your good reputation creates expectations for your good performance. If you have a good reputation, colleagues will think highly of you. The likelihood of your inclusion on important projects and on teams grows as your colleagues become confident that you will be a strong contributor.

Reputation and performance are two sides of the same coin. Good performance and a good reputation are built on your attitude, behavior, and production. Good performance feeds a great reputation and a great reputation bolsters good performance.

How Can Value Be Created in Your Organization?

A valuable employee is a good performer who creates value for his or her organization. Because some of your colleagues may feel that they know value when they see it, you need a more concrete definition around which to build activities and focus your efforts. In Chapter 12, we will look deeper at the following types of value that exist within your organization:

- Individual value
- Business value tied to internal financial drivers
- Business value tied to external marketplace drivers

The Three Mistakes You are Making Today

Deep within the heart of your organization's cubicle farm and hidden down hallways of closed office doors, you and dozens of your heads-down colleagues are working hard to stay employed. Our performance appraisal, metric-based culture has created generations of individuals like you who believe that good performance alone ensures job security. You believe that the attainment of a 4.2 on your annual performance appraisal and 100% completion of your MBOs (management by objectives) are the best strategies to employ to receive a promotion or avoid a layoff. At the same time, the importance of value creation in your organization continues to grow. Because no one or no behavior can guarantee you a job for life, you might be making one or all of the following mistakes as you navigate your organization:

- You are not creating value for your organization.
- If you are creating value, you and your boss are unable to describe it.
- You believe that good performance equals value.

The unemployment landscape is filled with high-performing individuals who thought that doing a great job, achieving their MBOs, and getting an "exceeds expectations" on their last performance appraisal would make all the difference. Today, a valuable employee is a good performer who creates value. She can tell stories about her good performance and the value she creates for her employer. Her boss and her organization *know* the value she creates.

WHY AREN'T YOU FOCUSED ON RAISING YOUR VALUE?

Carl does not realize it as it is happening, yet every day at work, he rationalizes that focusing on value has no room on his to-do list. When he takes a moment to think about raising his value, he convinces himself of one or more of the following:

- My good performance creates all the value I need to create for my organization.
- I don't know how to create value.
- I don't know what is valuable to my boss or my organization.
- My boss and my organization do not know what is valuable to the organization.
- No one wants me to create value. They just want me to get my job done.
- Why bother? The value that is important to my organization will just change.

Carl will tell colleagues who ask about his workday that he is very busy. He will reflect that he doesn't know where the time goes. He will be told by his boss that he is doing a great job. Does staying busy as weeks fly by make Carl valuable to his organization? *No, it doesn't!*

In the next chapter, you will see the different types of value that exist within organizations. You will see that there is plenty of value creation to go around. After all, what organization would not want all of their good performing employees to be actively seeking ways to add value to the organization?

Chapter Eleven Recap

- **Value** is when the outcome of a situation exceeds the cost incurred by a satisfactory margin.

- Despite what you hear from your organization's leaders, **today's organizations are not like a family.**

- In today's "get-it-done-yesterday" business environments, the frequency and pace of change is accelerating, tenure is shorter, and relationships are shallower.

- Getting an "exceeds expectations" on your annual performance appraisal is no longer enough; you must do more than just do your job well.

- You must be seen as a **valuable employee** – an employee who is a good performer and who creates value for your organization.

- **Costs** that can be incurred when creating value are the following:
  - Time
  - Energy
  - Money

- You **raise your value** with activities that connect individual contributions with business performance.

- The performance appraisal is an archaic tool that stifles value creation.

- The language being used to define success is slowly and quietly shifting from *performance* to *value*. Value is the new corporate currency!

- **Good performance** is defined as the factors that influence reputation - attitude, behavior, and production.

- Your good performance builds the perception of your good

reputation; your good reputation creates expectations of your good performance.

- You and your colleagues are making one or all of the following mistakes today:
  - You are not providing value to your organization.
  - You and your boss are unable to describe the value you currently create for your organization.
  - You believe that good performance equals value.
- You need to be a valuable employee and perceived to be a valuable employee to your organization – there is plenty of value to go around!

Chapter Twelve

Bring Value to Life

Carl is similar to you. He is working hard to stay afloat and stay ahead. Often he finds himself behind before the day has begun, and the avalanche of emails and flood of voicemails are not helping. His workplace is fast-paced and ever-changing. Carl hears his colleagues say things like "It's crazy around here!" When asked how they are doing, his colleagues almost always respond "Busy!" before he finishes asking his question.

You are very much like Carl. You have grown up in a culture focused on numerical ratings, bell curves, and annual performance assessments. You rush from meeting to meeting and conference call to conference call so blindly that months pass by before you open your eyes to see where all your rushing has taken you. You have little time to think about yourself. You defend "where you are" professionally by deluding yourself that being a good performer is enough. Yet, today's competitive and fast-paced workplaces are demanding more from business professionals like you and Carl. Your organization does not have the time or money to train you to be a good performer. As a stand-alone differentiator, good performance is no longer enough – it is expected!

You want to be more than a good performer – *you need to be a valuable employee.* You can't wait for others to come to your aid. In fact, no knight on a white horse is galloping his way to rescue you. Glinda, the Good Witch of the East, is not floating your way in her magic bubble to whisk you back to Kansas. The first step toward raising the value you create for your organization rests with you. You need to be the hero of your own story.

HOW IS VALUE CREATED IN ORGANIZATIONS?

There are many types of organizations in the world. Whether you work for a non-profit or for-profit, a manufacturer or a service provider, a "bricks and mortar" or virtual company, you work for an organization that *needs to survive* in a very competitive, fast-changing, and complex environment.

All organizations operating in complex environments are impacted by external and internal forces. Externally, your organization needs to raise capital in order to invest in its growth and generate revenue to cover its operating expenses with vendors and employees. In order for your organization to obtain capital or generate revenue, it needs to **create value** for investors and customers, as illustrated in Figure 12.1.

CREATING VALUE EXTERNALLY

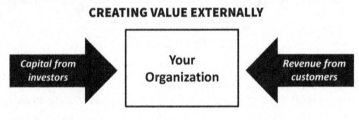

Figure 12.1

- **Investors.** Individual or institutional investors seek organizations that can create for themselves, or their clients, value in areas such as return on equity and earnings per share. These investors buy stock in your organization (i.e., a mutual fund), loan money to your organization (i.e., a bank), or invest in your organization (i.e., venture capitalist). Regardless of their function, these investors work hard to ensure value in their investment.

- **Customers.** Today's competitive marketplace demands that individuals and companies find the best price for the best product and service they seek. Whether it is a sophisticated consumer seeking value for clothing he is buying or a purchasing agent finding the best value in office products for her organization, buyers work to ensure value in their purchases. When customers find the value in the goods and services they are purchasing, they give your organization money, generating revenue.

Internally, your organization needs to be managed in ways that ensure investors and customers stay interested. In order for your organization to survive for the long-term, it needs to **obtain value** from vendors and employees, as illustrated in Figure 12.2.

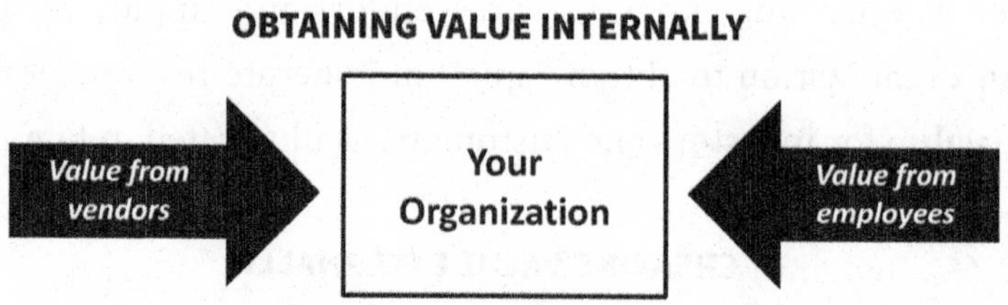

OBTAINING VALUE INTERNALLY

Figure 12.2

There are numerous variables your organization manages internally to keep external stakeholders interested through value creation. One of the most significant ways to create value internally is by managing expenses with vendors and employees.

- **Vendors.** In order to manage expenses well, your colleagues work with vendors to find the best price for the best product or service to fulfill budget expectations and support margin objectives. Whether it is airline tickets, benefit plans, paper clips, or coffee, you and your organization take on the role of a customer, just like the external customer described previously.

- **Employees.** Today's fast-paced and competitive marketplaces demand that organizations remain nimble and creative, increase revenue while reducing costs, and change frequently. In order to achieve these challenging objectives, organizations need you focused on creating value. Good performance, is expected

– you must contribute more than just doing your job well. Your organization needs you to focus on activities (i.e., managing expenses) that connect your contributions to your organization's business performance.

VALUE CREATION IS FINANCIALLY BASED

In the *Raise Your Visibility & Value* model, **value** is defined as the outcome of a situation when the outcome of a situation exceeds the cost incurred by a satisfactory margin. **Raising your value** is defined as performing activities that connect individual contributions with business performance. To be considered a valuable employee, you must tie as many of your activities as possible to how your organization measures how well it's performing. For most organizations, business performance is predominantly measured through financial performance, as illustrated in Figure 12.3. As you work to create value for your organization, you must focus your activities on your company's financial performance.

THE FOCUS OF INDIVIDUAL CONTRIBUTIONS

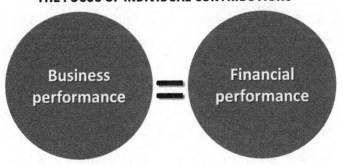

Figure 12.3

Why must value creation be tied to your organization's financial performance? While the foundations of a family are its historical, legal and genetic connections, the foundation of an organization rests in its financials. Your organization needs revenue in order to survive. Concurrently, your organization needs to manage its expenses effectively.

Finance, like other business disciplines, has a language all its own, and this book is not intended to be a primer on business finance. Yet, you should know the following: Without a doubt nothing will end a well-meaning Human Resources initiative, the rollout of a new technology infrastructure, or the purchase of a much-needed fleet of trucks than a drop in revenue or an unexpected expense. Nothing short of a natural disaster will impact the activities that are important to you and your organization more than the direction of your organization's finances.

Hence, financial management offers the greatest opportunity to create value in your organization. Good performers do their jobs well and expect that their good performance will make a positive impact on their organization. Valuable employees do their jobs well and connect their individual contributions with business performance.

WHAT TYPES OF VALUE CAN I CREATE FOR MY ORGANIZATION?

In order for an organization to obtain value from you and for you to raise your value within your organization, you must capitalize on either an existing way of creating value or identify new ways to create value. You can create value in your organization in the following ways:

- By continuing value creation in ways that are already **existing**.
  - For example, recognizing that a high number of product returns are due to owners not understanding how to use Product A (versus Product A being defective), you consistently use a script *your employer created* to educate customers on the correct use of Product A, thus reducing the number of products returned by customers.
- By creating value in ways that are **new.**
  - For example, recognizing that a high number of product returns are due to Product A being defective, you *create a script* to help educate customers on a revised use of Product A, thus reducing the number of products returned by customers.

- By creating value in ways that are **different.**
  - For example, recognizing that a high number of product returns also exist for Product B, you *create an updated script* to help educate customers on the correct use of the Products A and B, thus reducing the number of products being returned.

The types of value that you can create for your organization are endless. As a business professional you must seek ways to distinguish yourself in your frenetic work environment, to strengthen your job security, and to minimize the likelihood of an adverse job action, you must seek ways to demonstrate the value you can create for your organization is crucial.

In What Ways Can Value be Created?

In the *Raise Your Visibility & Value* model, value creation is segmented into the following value types, as illustrated in Figure 12.4:

1. Individual value
2. Business value tied to internal financial drivers
3. Business value tied to external marketplace drivers

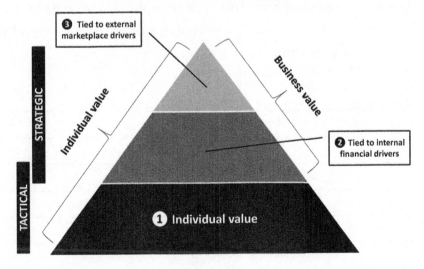

VALUE CREATION SEGMENTS

Figure 12.4

1. Individual Value

When you perform your job well, you are valuable to your organization. When you are focused primarily on creating individual value, you tend to be in a role that is more tactically-focused. And let's face it, some roles in organizations need to be tactically focused and this focus is very valuable to the organization. Not every role has a clear line of sight to financial performance, nor should they. At the same time, most organizations have yet to explore how roles, even the most tactical, can create value to the organization by exploring how individuals within these roles can impact financial performance. Not all value that is created has to be worth millions of dollars, or qualify for the cover of *Time* magazine. Even individuals in a tactical role or a group of individuals comprising a function can create value for the organization.

Recognition of performance-based individual value generally occurs through a performance appraisal process and is one of the reasons that performance management systems will continue to exist. These appraisals are highlighted by behaviors such as "adaptable," "flexible," and "timely." These behaviors are also very similar to the words used to describe a good reputation (Chapter 10) and good performance (Chapter 11).

In the spaces below, list some of the terms or phrases your organization uses on its current performance appraisal to measure performance. I've listed one example below.

Adaptable _____   _____

_____   _____

_____   _____

_____   _____

_____   _____

2. Business value tied to internal financial drivers

Like an adolescent transitioning to adulthood, growing and evolving organizations require value to be more tangible, and the contribution of business value by employees to be broader. While individual value is critically important to an organization's performance and culture, it is not the type of value that will sustain an organization in its marketplace. Business value tied to internal financial drivers reflects a more strategic perspective that can have a positive impact on your organization. In today's competitive marketplaces, your organization needs as many employees as possible focused on creating value through internal financial drivers.

As you work to raise your value, start with identifying the financial performance drivers that are important to your organization. Internal financial drivers vary from organization to organization and may include revenue, sales, expenses, gross margin, gross profit, key performance indicators, key financial ratios, and profit margin.

If you do not know what these internal financial drivers are, there are a number of ways to identify them:

- Partner with a colleague to brainstorm.
- Listen to the areas on which your leaders discuss during your next all-employee meeting.
- As you work to raise your visibility with your boss or key leaders at least two levels above you (Chapter 7), ask them to identify the key financial drivers for your organization.
- Read your organization's annual report and listen in on its next investor call.

The best way to know what financial drivers are important to your organization is to look at what is reported to the public and investors.

In the spaces below, list some of the internal financial drivers that are important to your organization. I've listed one example below.

<u>Sales per hour</u>_____   _____

_____   _____

_____   _____

_____   _____

When you have a better understanding of the financial drivers that are important to your organization, you are in a better position to identify ways to impact them. If, after exploring ways to impact internal financial drivers, you find that there is no logical way to do so, you may be in a role better suited to create individual value. Do not make any assumptions – value can be created in a variety of ways and you will not know the value you can create until you conduct this exploration.

3.   Business value tied to external marketplace drivers

The competitive global marketplace shows little mercy for organizations that are slow to raise the bar for their customers and their employees. Business value tied to external marketplace drivers tend to be strategically focused and is created by:

- Anticipating changes in the marketplace.
- Building decision alternatives based on a variety of implications (i.e., financial, cultural, geographic).
- Considering risk in strategic decisions.
- Taking action that has broad and long-term implications.

Realistically, fewer roles within your organization will be focused on external marketplace drivers. These roles are focused primarily on strategy - looking around the corner to see what is coming before it comes, and knowing where to go before others get there. These roles possess some degree of individual value, as all roles do, and some degree of business value tied to internal financial drivers. Yet, the majority of the focus of these roles is on broader, long-term outcomes. External marketplace drivers are typically segmented into two core areas:

- **Economic drivers -** inflation, interest rates, insurance rates, unemployment, new housing starts, and retail sales.
- **Competitive drivers -** strategies of competitors, buyer alternatives, and advances in technology.

In the spaces below, list some of the drivers tied to the external marketplace that are important to your organization.

Insurance premiums

_____   _____

_____   _____

_____   _____

How Do I Start Raising My Value?

With so many options and possibilities already existing in your organization, you can start raising your value immediately. Before you jump out of your chair and begin the shift from good performer to valuable employee, however, you need to do the following two things:

- **Host a conversation with your boss** on how to create value for your organization. Recall that no relationship is more important in your frenetic working environment than the relationship you have with your boss. How you create value for your organization has to be supported by your boss. Providing value in ways that are not wanted or "authorized" will get you nowhere fast. Your boss can be a great partner in helping you become a valuable employee.
- **Conduct a value identification exercise.** You may find that some of your activities are currently creating value for your organization. You may also find that some are close to creating

value, while others are just doing busy-work and not providing any value at all. In your fast-paced work environment, you are being asked to do more with less, and do more faster. Although you may have been busy, you may find that your activities have not created value for your organization. By conducting a value identification exercise now, you can confirm if your activities create value for your organization or not - before anyone else does!

How do I Conduct a Value Identification Exercise?

Take a moment to think about a key activity/project in which you are currently engaged. Then take a few moments to review Figure 12.5 and complete a value identification exercise for this activity or project. An activity tends to be smaller and completed on a recurring basis, while a project tends to be larger and done only once. An effective strategy in completing your value identification exercise is to find a colleague who can help you think through this important information. Think about the following:

- **What is the name of this activity/project?** All activities should have a name so you can easily reference the activity when speaking with others. Give the activity a brief name that will be clear to just about anyone, unless it is a highly confidential project that warrants a code name.

- **How would you briefly describe the activity to others?** Your colleagues do not have time to listen to lengthy, rambling, confusing descriptions. As Albert Einstein said, "If you can't explain it simply, you don't understand it well enough." Create a tight description of what you are doing.

- **What is/are the business problem(s) this activity will solve?** All solutions start with a problem. If you do not know the specific problem you are solving, you may end up with the wrong solution.

Develop a tight description of the business problem your activity will solve.

- **What does success for this activity look like?** In his book, *The 7 Habits of Effective People,* Stephen Covey identified "Start with the end in mind" as a proven effective habit.[1] Create a compelling, exciting, visionary-like outcome for your activity to keep colleagues engaged and interested.

- **What is/are the risk(s) of doing this activity?** Any change can create ripples in your work environment that may be risky. This is the way things are. Not anticipating and planning for these risks can be problematic. Identify the risks associated with doing this activity.

- **What is/are the risk(s) of not doing this activity?** There is an expectation that not doing an activity or project is riskier than doing it. Identify the risks associated with not doing this activity to ensure they are greater than the risks of doing it.

- **What financial driver(s) will this activity impact?** In order for the activity to create business value, there must be one or more financial drivers positively impacted. These drivers may be tied to internal financial or external marketplace drivers. Identify the financial driver(s) that you are seeking to impact that makes the investment of time, energy, and money in your activity worthwhile and valuable to your organization.

- **Can the financial benefit be estimated and, if so, what is it?** In order for the value of the activity to be prioritized against other activities that are competing for your organization's time, energy, and money, you need to estimate the financial benefit that your activity will generate for your organization. Your estimate needs to be based on tangible facts and reasonable assumptions. If identifying a hard number is not possible, at least provide a range representing the positive impact that your activity will generate.

VALUE IDENTIFICATION EXERCISE

What is the name of the activity?	How would you briefly describe the activity to others?	What is the business problem this activity will solve?	What does success for this activity look like?	What is the risk(s) of doing this activity?	What is the risk(s) of not doing this activity?	What financial driver(s) will this activity impact?	What is the actual or estimated financial benefit of this activity?

Figure 12.5

You can download this form at the *Raise Your Visibility & Value* link at the www.excellius.com website.

How Do I Host a Value Conversation with My Boss?

As stated previously, there is no greater activity to begin the process of raising the value you create for your organization than a conversation with your boss about value creation. By approaching your boss and requesting a conversation regarding value creation, you are already raising your value in your organization. Yet, at the same time, *this is not a conversation being held in organizations across the globe.* Hence, when responding to your request, your boss may be:

- **Confused.** Since value creation conversations are not yet common in organizations, your boss may be confused by your request or not understand your motives. To help reduce confusion, review the talking points shown below in the "At Your Value Meeting Steps and Talking Points" section.

- **Surprised.** Your boss may be surprised to see this new side of you! Talking about value is a feel-good exercise and the conversation can generate a lot of positive energy and excitement. Capitalize on your boss's feeling of excitement and encourage her to join you in this important conversation.

- **Dismissive.** Some bosses may not know what to do with this new topic. In ever-changing workplaces, it is easy to dismiss new topics or delay them until a later point in time. Don't let your boss dismiss this topic too quickly; and, if she does, take the opportunity to bring it up again at a later date.

Since this is not a conversation being held widely in organizations, you need to be the following in order to make progress on this vital topic:

- **Be Courageous.** Depending on the stories you are telling yourself on where you fit in your organization and the degree of value you have been providing, the value creation conversation may take some courage. As you put yourself "out there," you might fear that your boss's response to "What value do I create for our organization?" may be "None!" As value creation is a feel-good topic, the likelihood of this is minimal. The talking points shown below ensure that your goals are clear and that the outcome of the conversation is beneficial to you. This may not be an easy conversation to have, so be courageous.

- **Be Persistent.** You may find that your boss is not sure how to participate in a conversation regarding value creation or your boss may be dismissive. More likely, in your jam-packed, fast-paced, ever-changing business environments, there may never seem to be a good time. This is a conversation worth having, so be persistent.

- **Be Patient.** You may find that your value creation conversation with your boss might take multiple meetings over a period of time. This is a new conversation, so be patient.

When you are ready to have a conversation with your boss regarding how you can create value for your organization, you can follow certain steps to ensure that you have a healthy and productive conversation.

STEPS TO TAKE BEFORE YOUR VALUE MEETING

1. Identify the business performance drivers that are important to your organization. Brainstorm with a colleague, speak with a senior leader, or talk with someone in finance, sales, business development, or operations.

2. Complete the **value identification exercise.** Identify value that you currently create or could create. You can also work with a colleague or friend to help you think through the exercise and challenge your thinking.

3. Schedule a time with your boss in advance. Make it clear in your invitation that you are requesting the meeting to be solely focused on discussing business value. (Use some of the talking points in

the "Steps to Take and Talking Points to Make During Your Value Meeting" section that follows in order to be clear with your boss on the focus of the meeting.)

4. If appropriate, consider sending your value identification exercise in advance for your boss to preview.

STEPS TO TAKE AND TALKING POINTS TO MAKE DURING YOUR VALUE MEETING

1. Consider saying something like the following to get the conversation going:

   - "Thank you for finding time to speak with me about the value I create for our organization."

   - "I appreciate the information that was shared in my last performance appraisal and I am continuing to focus on the areas of opportunity that we have identified."

   - "In addition to improving my performance over time, I am also interested in creating value for our organization."

   - "By focusing on value as well as good performance, I think I can grow as a contributor and have a greater impact on our company's success."

   - "By value, I specifically mean activities that connect my performance to the business performance of our organization."

   - "I recognize this is a new conversation for us and I am excited that we can explore this topic together."

   - "I'd like to share some thoughts to start our conversation (value identification exercise), and I hope we can build from there."

   - "What are your thoughts?"

2. Acknowledge that this conversation may require multiple meetings in order to make meaningful progress.

3. Close the meeting by ensuring that the next steps are clear to you and your boss.

4. Thank your boss for her time and insights.

STEPS TO TAKE AFTER YOUR VALUE MEETING

1. Send a recap of your conversation (i.e., what you heard, next steps) to your boss.

2. If appropriate, schedule a follow-up meeting to continue the conversation and to ensure that you keep making progress.

3. Focus on the next steps that move you closer to connecting your contributions with the business's performance.

Chapter Twelve Recap

- Externally, your organization needs to raise capital in order to invest in its growth and generate revenue to cover its operating expenses. In order for your organization to obtain capital or generate revenue, it needs to **create value** for investors and customers.

- Internally, your organization needs to manage its finances (i.e., manage expenses.) In order for your organization to survive for the long-term, it needs to **obtain value** from vendors and employees.

- **Value creation** is financially based. Nothing short of a natural disaster will impact the investment of time, energy, and money in activities that are important to you and your organization more than the direction of your organization's finances.

- You can **create value** in new, exciting, and visionary ways:
  - Existing
  - New
  - Different

- You can **create value** within the following segments:
  - Individual value
  - Business value tied to internal financial drivers
  - Business value tied to external marketplace drivers

- **Individual value** exists for good performers whose connection to the financial drivers of their organization is limited.

- Positively impacting revenue, expenses, and profit margin is examples of creating business value for your organization that is tied to **internal financial drivers**.

- Identifying favorable interest rates, negotiating lower insurance premiums, and anticipating competitor strategies are examples of creating business value for your organization tied to **external marketplace drivers**.

- Start creating value for your organization by doing the following two activities:

  - Conduct a **value identification exercise.**

  - Host a **value conversation** with your boss.

Chapter Thirteen

Be the Catalyst of Your Own Career!

By all accounts, the world of work you are experiencing is significantly different than your parents' world of work. The old ways of networking and measuring performance are ineffective in the face of unprecedented change and transparency.

Now is the time to differentiate yourself in your organization and industry. Now is the time to move beyond networking and start raising your visibility. Now is the time to break your dependency on performance management systems and start raising your value.

The first step begins with you. This may be a short hop for some of you; for others, it may be a longer journey. Regardless of the length of your stride, keep in mind two important areas of context to increase the likelihood of your success - **pace** and **practice.** Not all progress occurs overnight – that's why we call it progress. **Pace** yourself as you work with the ideas you created in your *Visibility Activity Map*. Your progress doesn't have to be perfect or unfold in ways exactly as you planned, yet it is still progress. At the same time, **practice** purposefully so you can enjoy your progress. You can use this insight to motivate you to raise your visibility and value in your organization and industry. If you aren't practicing raising your visibility and value, somewhere, somebody else is; and when you come head-to-head with her when being considered for a job, a promotion or, a raise, she will prevail.

Take a moment to identify your first step in **raising your visibility** in your organization and industry. Your first step could be to schedule time with a colleague to strategize how to raise your visibility. Perhaps you aspire to meet a senior leader two levels above you in your chain of command. Maybe you are ready to contribute an article for your company blog. Chapters 2 – 10 are filled with ideas that you can use to take the first step. So, what is your first step?

---

*MY FIRST STEP TO **RAISE** MY **VISIBILITY** IN MY ORGANIZATION IS TO*

_____

_____

_____

---

*MY FIRST STEP TO **RAISE** MY **VISIBILITY** IN MY INDUSTRY IS TO*

_____

_____

_____

Now, take a moment to identify your first step in **raising your value** in your organization. Is it a value conversation with your boss? Is it to identify the business drivers that are important to your organization? Chapters 11 and 12 can help jumpstart your thinking. What is your first step?

*MY FIRST STEP TO **RAISE** MY **VALUE** IN MY ORGANIZATION IS TO*

_____

_____

_____

Congratulations! You have begun the process of regaining control over your career and enriching your work experience. As we part, my wishes for you, your career, and your success mirror the goals found in the *Introduction* of this book.

- Realize that networking as you define it today is no longer enough for you to achieve your professional objectives.

- Understand that performance management systems hinder your ability to differentiate yourself within your organization.

- Create activities that will help you move beyond networking and **raise your visibility** in your organization and industry.

- Create activities that will help you avoid the limitations of performance appraisals and **raise your value** in your organization.

- Increase your satisfaction in the work that you do and your engagement in your organization's goals and mission.

Charles Edward "Ed" McCauley was an NBA player (1949 – 1959) with the St. Louis Bombers and the Boston Celtics and coach (1958 – 1960) for the St. Louis Hawks. As a star player in a frenetic and ever-changing environment, McCauley knew the value of practice. "When you are not practicing," McCauley said, "somewhere, somebody else is; and when you meet him, he will win!"

Be the catalyst of your own career! Now is the time to raise your visibility and value in your organization and industry. Now is the time to take your first step.

Notes

Raise Your Visibility & Value Footnotes

1. Lost last episode, 2005 – 2010, produced by ABC Studios.

Introduction

1. Reller, Tami, as quoted by Shira Ovide, "Microsoft Concedes Windows 8 Struggles," *Wall Street Journal*, May 8, 2013.

2. United States Department of Labor Statistics - http://data.bls.gov/timeseries/LNS14000000.

3. Johns Hopkins University Career Center handout on networking - http://pages.jh.edu/~careers/students/handouts/networking.pdf. This is also consistent with information shared by outplacement firms across the United States.

Chapter 1 – Why Networking and Performance Appraisals Are Not Enough

1. Maslow, A. H., "The Theory of Human Motivation, *Psychological Review*, 1943. Maslow wanted to understand what motivates people. He believed that people possess a set of motivation systems unrelated to rewards or unconscious desires. Maslow stated that people are motivated to achieve certain needs. When one need is fulfilled a person seeks to fulfill the next one, and so on. The earliest and most widespread version of Maslow's (1943, 1954) *hierarchy of needs* includes five motivational needs, often depicted as hierarchical levels within a pyramid. This five-stage model can be divided into basic (or deficiency) needs (e.g. physiological, safety, love, and esteem) and growth needs (self-actualization).

2. Details from a poll I conducted on LinkedIn as shown below.

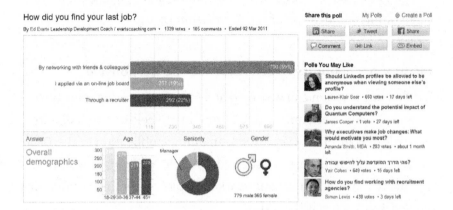

3. This is the result of an informal poll I took with colleagues as I was networking between the months of June and September 2008.

4. HR.BLR.com infographic on performance appraisal system effectiveness, http://hr.blr.com/HR-news/Performance-Termination/ Performance-Employee-Appraisal/Infographic-2014-employee-performance-appraisal-pr#, 2014.

5. 99.9% of the world's population do not like performance appraisals. While this may feel like an exaggeration, over my twenty-four year career in Human Resources, this is the most accurate number I have.

6. There is no survey to support that people like pigs with lipstick more than completing a performance appraisal. The word survey is being used colloquially.

7. This information can be found in the March 2014 *Inc. Magazine* analysis on organizational change, looking at how different your company is today than it was five years ago.

8. Rometty, Virginia, Chief Executive Officer, IBM, "IBM's Chief to Employees: Think Fast, Move Faster", *Wall Street Journal*, April 24, 2013.

9. This information can be found at http://www.manhattandigest. com/2013/12/09/singularity-dont-know-start-paying-attention/, an online publication of the *Manhattan Digest*.

Chapter 6 – Visibility Accelerator #3 – Be Responsive

1. This information can be found at a May 2011 posting on http:// www.deadzones.com/2011/05/how-many-cell-phone-calls-are-made-day.html#.VRVqi_nF8f4, an online publication of the *Dead Zones*, which discusses issues with AT&T, Verizon, T-Mobile, Sprint and Tracfone. Four years have passed, so this number has clearly grown significantly.

2. Email Statistics Report, 2011 – 2015, The Radicati Group, Palo Alto, CA.

Chapter 7 – Visibility Accelerator #4 - Interact with Others

1. Kamenetz, Anya, The Four Year Career, Fast Company, http:// www.fastcompany.com/1802731/four-year-career , 2011.

Chapter 10 – Visibility Accelerator #10 - Manage Your Reputation

1. Hoffman, Reid and Casnocha, Ben "The Start-Up of You", *Crown Business Publishing*, 2012.

Chapter 11 – Raise Your Value

1. Netflix Culture: Freedom and Responsibility, http://www.slide-share.net/reed2001/culture-1798664, slide 23, 2009

2. Ibarra, Herminia, "Why Managers Are Stuck in Their Silos," *Wall Street Journal*, April 28, 2014.

3. Ibarra, Herminia, "Why Managers Are Stuck in Their Silos," *Wall Street Journal*, April 28, 2014.

Chapter 12 – Bring Value to Life

1. Covey, Stephen R., "The 7 Habits of Highly Effective People", Simon & Schuster, 1989

CPSIA information can be obtained
at www.ICGtesting.com
Printed in the USA
BVOW09*2244011017
496155BV00001B/1/P